MASTERING LEADERSHIP WITHOUT AUTHORITY

A Strategic Guide to Amplifying Your Impact

WILLIE A. MULLINS

© 2024 Willie A. Mullins.

All rights reserved. No part of this book may be reproduced, distributed, or transmitted in any form or by any means, including photocopying, recording, or other electronic or mechanical methods, without the prior written permission of the author, except in the case of brief quotations embodied in critical reviews and certain other non-commercial uses permitted by copyright law. For permission requests, write to the publisher at the address below.

Disclaimer:

The information in this book is based on the author's personal experience, research, and views on leadership. The contents are intended for educational and informational purposes only and should not be construed as professional advice. The author and publisher make no representations or warranties regarding the accuracy, applicability, or completeness of the contents of this book. Readers are advised to consult appropriate professionals before making any decisions based on the information provided herein. The author and publisher disclaim any liability for any direct or indirect loss or damage arising from the use or application of the contents of this book.

TABLE OF CONTENTS

Introduction	7
Part I: Building the Foundation	**11**
Identifying Your Leadership Strengths	11
The Influence of Middle Management	20
Creating Strategic Impact without Authority	27
Leveraging Relationships for Success	27
Understanding Organizational Dynamics	47
Mastering Communication: The Key to Influence	57
Persuasive Communication Techniques	57
Listening and Feedback Loops	74
Part II: Cultivating Personal Leadership	**93**
Developing Discipline and Self-Motivation	93
Creating a Personal Leadership Plan	134
Emotional Intelligence and Leadership	142
Harnessing EI for Effective Leadership	142
Managing Stress and Building Resilience	150
Critical Thinking for Leaders	159
Methods for Analyzing Situations Objectively	160

Decision-Making without Formal Authority	170

Part III: Leading and Inspiring Teams — 180

Techniques for Fostering Team Collaboration	180
Encouraging Initiative and Accountability	192
Building Trust and Respect among Peers	201
Establishing Credibility in Non-Leadership Roles	201
Handling Conflicts with Diplomacy	209
Driving Change without Being in Charge	218
Strategies for Influencing Organizational Change	218
Leading Innovation from Any Position	227

Part IV: Navigating Organizational Challenges — 247

Effective Upward Communication Techniques	247
Building a Strong Rapport with Leadership	252
Overcoming Common Challenges of Non-Title Leadership	265
Handling Resistance and Pushback	265
Balancing Authority and Collaboration	274

Part V: Sustaining Long-Term Leadership — 281

Developing a Growth Mindset	281

Staying Adaptable in a Changing Environment	290
Measuring the Impact of Your Leadership	298
Tools for Self-Assessment and Reflection	298
Creating a Legacy without Formal Authority	308

Conclusion: **317**

INTRODUCTION

Imagine walking into a room filled with decision-makers, each holding the power to shape the future of your organization. You don't have a title that commands authority, yet the room quiets as you begin to speak. Why? Because leadership isn't about titles it's about influence. In today's dynamic and ever-changing work environment, the ability to lead without formal authority is not just an asset; it's a necessity. Whether you're a seasoned manager or an emerging professional, the power of influence allows you to guide, motivate, and inspire others, regardless of your position in the hierarchy. This book is about unlocking that power.

Leadership has traditionally been associated with titles, but in reality, titles alone don't make leaders. True leadership is defined by influence the ability to affect change and guide others toward a shared vision. This influence doesn't come from a job title; it's earned through trust, credibility, and the ability to connect with others. Think about some of the most impactful leaders in history figures like Martin Luther King Jr., Mahatma Gandhi, or even more contemporary leaders like Malala Yousafzai. None of them relied on a formal title to lead. Their influence was built on the strength of their convictions, their ability to inspire, and their unwavering commitment to a cause greater than themselves.

In the modern workplace, influence is more critical than ever. Organizations are increasingly adopting flatter structures, where collaboration and cross-functional teams are the norm. In such environments, the ability to lead without relying on formal authority is essential. This book will show you how to develop that influence, enabling you to lead effectively, regardless of your official role.

Having spent years studying and working with leaders at all levels, I've seen firsthand the difference between those who rely on their title and those who lead with influence. The latter are the ones who truly make a difference they are the leaders who inspire action, drive change, and leave a lasting impact. The core thesis of this book is simple: Leadership isn't about the position you hold; it's about the influence you wield. Throughout this book, you will learn how to harness the power of influence to lead effectively in any situation, even when you don't have formal authority.

In the chapters that follow, we will explore the essential components of influence and how they apply to leadership. We'll start by building a strong foundation, understanding your role in leading from the middle, and mastering the art of communication. From there, we'll delve into personal leadership, focusing on self-discipline, emotional intelligence, and critical thinking. We'll then shift our focus to leading and inspiring teams, navigating organizational challenges, and sustaining long-term leadership. Each section is filled with practical strategies, real-world examples, and actionable insights to help you become a more influential leader.

But this book is more than just theory. You'll find stories of leaders who have successfully navigated the challenges of leading without authority stories that will inspire you to take action and apply these principles in your own life. You'll discover that influence can be more powerful than authority, and that by mastering it, you can achieve extraordinary results.

Let me share a story that captures the essence of influence in leadership. A few years ago, I worked with a team at a mid-sized tech company. There was a young engineer named Sarah who didn't hold a managerial position, but she had a knack for rallying her team around new ideas. Despite not having a formal title, Sarah became the go-to person for critical projects. Her influence grew, not because she demanded it, but because she earned it through her dedication, expertise, and the genuine respect of her peers. Sarah's story is a testament to the power of influence it's about leading with your actions, your words, and your values.

Some of you might be thinking, "But I'm not in a leadership position, so how can this apply to me?" The beauty of influence is that it transcends titles. Whether you're leading a team, managing a project, or simply working within a group, your ability to influence others is what sets you apart. This book will give you the tools to harness that influence, no matter where you are in your career.

As you turn the pages of this book, you'll embark on a journey to understand and master the art of influence. You'll learn that true leadership is not confined by a title or position; it's defined by your ability to inspire, motivate, and guide others. So, let's begin this journey together toward becoming the leader who doesn't need a title to make a difference.

BONUS INCLUDED IN THE CONCLUSION PAGE

PART I: BUILDING THE FOUNDATION

UNDERSTANDING YOUR ROLE: LEADING FROM THE MIDDLE

As a leadership coach, one of the most significant aspects of helping individuals in middle management is guiding them in identifying and leveraging their unique leadership strengths. Middle managers often find themselves at the crossroads of organizational operations, responsible for bridging the gap between upper management's strategic vision and the day-to-day execution by frontline employees. In this vital role, understanding and utilizing personal leadership strengths can dramatically enhance their effectiveness, allowing them to lead with confidence and positively impact their teams and the organization as a whole.

IDENTIFYING YOUR LEADERSHIP STRENGTHS

Leadership strengths are the inherent qualities, skills, and attributes that enable individuals to inspire, guide, and motivate others toward achieving common goals. These strengths can be categorized into various domains, such as communication, decision-making, emotional intelligence, strategic thinking, and more. Recognizing and honing these strengths is crucial for middle managers, as they often navigate complex interpersonal dynamics, drive team performance, and implement organizational strategies.

The process of identifying leadership strengths involves introspection, feedback, and practical assessment. It's about understanding what you naturally excel at and how those abilities can be applied to lead more effectively.

Step 1: Self-Reflection and Introspection

The first step in identifying leadership strengths is self-reflection. This involves taking a deep and honest look at oneself, examining past experiences, successes, and challenges to uncover the qualities that consistently contribute to positive outcomes.

Begin by asking yourself the following questions:

- ❖ What are the tasks or responsibilities that I consistently perform well?
- ❖ In what situations do I feel most confident and capable as a leader?
- ❖ Which of my actions have had the most significant positive impact on my team or organization?
- ❖ What feedback have I received from peers, subordinates, or superiors regarding my leadership style?

For example, if you find that you naturally excel in crisis situations, remaining calm and making quick, effective decisions, this might indicate a strength in decision-making under pressure. Alternatively, if your team members frequently seek your guidance and value your mentorship, you may have strong interpersonal and coaching skills.

Step 2: Seek Feedback from Others

While self-reflection is essential, it's equally important to seek feedback from others to gain a well-rounded understanding of your leadership strengths. Often, colleagues, team members, and superiors can provide valuable insights into how your leadership is perceived and where your strengths lie.

Consider implementing a 360-degree feedback process, where you gather input from a variety of sources, including:

- Direct reports who can speak to your day-to-day leadership.
- Peers who can provide insights into your collaborative abilities.
- Supervisors who can assess your performance from a strategic perspective.

When collecting feedback, ask specific questions that focus on identifying strengths. For instance:

- ❖ What do you see as my greatest strengths in leading the team?
- ❖ In which areas do you believe I have the most impact as a leader?
- ❖ Can you provide examples of when my leadership made a significant difference?

Feedback from others can reveal patterns that you may not have noticed. For instance, if multiple people mention your ability to motivate others during challenging times, this could indicate a strength in inspirational leadership.

Step 3: Assessing Leadership Strengths through Formal Tools

To supplement self-reflection and feedback, consider using formal assessment tools designed to identify leadership strengths. These tools can provide a structured approach to understanding your abilities and how they align with effective leadership.

Some commonly used leadership assessment tools include:

StrengthsFinder: This tool helps individuals discover their top strengths out of 34 possible themes. It's widely used in organizations to help leaders focus on their most potent qualities.

Myers-Briggs Type Indicator (MBTI): MBTI helps individuals understand their personality type and how it influences their leadership style, decision-making, and interactions with others.

Emotional Intelligence (EQ) Assessments: Tools like the EQ-i 2.0 assess emotional intelligence, which is crucial for effective leadership, particularly in managing relationships and understanding others' emotions.

Using these assessments, you can gain deeper insights into your leadership profile. For example, if StrengthsFinder reveals that one of your top strengths is "Communication," you might focus on becoming an even more effective communicator by enhancing your ability to articulate vision, provide feedback, and inspire your team.

Step 4: Aligning Strengths with Organizational Goals

Once you have identified your leadership strengths, the next step is to align them with your organization's goals and objectives. This alignment ensures that your strengths contribute directly to your team's success and the broader organizational mission.

Start by understanding the key strategic goals of your organization. Then, reflect on how your strengths can help achieve these goals. For example:

If your organization is focused on innovation, and you have a strength in creative thinking, you might take the lead in brainstorming sessions or champion new initiatives.

If the goal is to improve customer satisfaction, and you excel in building relationships, you might focus on enhancing client interactions and fostering a customer-centric culture within your team.

By aligning your strengths with organizational goals, you position yourself as a key contributor to the company's success, making your leadership both impactful and strategic.

Step 5: Developing and Enhancing Leadership Strengths

Identifying strengths is just the beginning; the next crucial step is to develop and enhance these strengths continually. Leadership is an ongoing journey of growth and improvement, and even your strongest attributes can be refined.

Here are some strategies for developing leadership strengths:

Seek Out Challenging Opportunities: Take on projects or roles that challenge your strengths and push you out of your comfort zone. For example, if you're strong in strategic thinking, volunteer to lead a long-term planning project that requires complex problem-solving and foresight.

Engage in Continuous Learning: Attend workshops, seminars, or courses related to your strengths. If communication is your strength, for instance, you might benefit from advanced public speaking or negotiation courses.

Find a Mentor: A mentor who excels in your areas of strength can provide valuable guidance, share experiences, and offer feedback as you work to enhance your abilities.

Reflect and Iterate: Regularly assess your progress in developing your strengths. Reflect on what's working well and where there's room for improvement, and adjust your approach accordingly.

Step 6: Leveraging Leadership Strengths in Middle Management

Middle managers are uniquely positioned to influence both the strategic direction set by upper management and the operational execution by frontline employees. Leveraging your leadership strengths in this role is crucial to driving organizational success.

Consider these strategies to apply your strengths effectively:

Influence Upward and Downward: Use your strengths to bridge the gap between upper management and your team. For instance, if you're strong in communication, ensure that the strategic vision from leadership is clearly communicated to your team, while also effectively conveying your team's feedback and concerns to higher-ups.

Mentor and Develop Others: If coaching is one of your strengths, use it to mentor and develop your team members. This not only enhances their performance but also builds a culture of growth and learning within your department.

Lead by Example: Leverage your strengths to set a positive example for your team. For instance, if you excel in decision-making, demonstrate how to make informed, timely decisions in challenging situations, thereby setting a standard for others to follow.

Drive Innovation and Change: Use your strengths to lead initiatives that drive innovation and change. If strategic thinking is your forte, take the lead in proposing and implementing new ideas that align with the company's goals.

Common Leadership Strengths and Their Development

Let's explore some common leadership strengths and how they can be developed further:

Communication: Effective communication is a cornerstone of leadership. To develop this strength, focus on improving both verbal and written communication skills. Practice active listening, ensure clarity in your messaging, and work on your ability to persuade and inspire others.

Emotional Intelligence: Emotional intelligence involves understanding and managing your own emotions and those of others. To enhance this strength, engage in mindfulness practices, seek feedback on your interpersonal interactions, and continually work on your empathy and relationship-building skills.

Decision-Making: Strong decision-making involves evaluating options, considering risks, and choosing the best course of action. To develop this strength, practice making decisions in various scenarios, seek input from diverse perspectives, and learn from both successful and unsuccessful outcomes.

Strategic Thinking: Strategic thinkers can see the big picture and plan for the future. To build this strength, stay informed about industry trends, engage in long-term planning exercises, and collaborate with others to brainstorm innovative solutions to complex problems.

Adaptability: In a rapidly changing environment, adaptability is crucial. To develop this strength, embrace change, remain open to new ideas, and cultivate a flexible mindset that allows you to pivot when necessary.

THE INFLUENCE OF MIDDLE MANAGEMENT

Middle management plays a crucial role in the success of any organization, serving as the bridge between the strategic vision set by upper management and the operational execution carried out by frontline employees. Despite not being at the top of the hierarchy, middle managers wield significant influence and can drive meaningful change within their teams and the broader organization. Understanding the impact of middle management is essential to appreciating how these individuals contribute to organizational success.

Understanding the Role of Middle Management

Middle managers typically oversee specific departments, projects, or teams within an organization. Their primary responsibilities include implementing the strategies and policies set by senior leadership, managing day-to-day operations, and ensuring that their teams meet performance targets. However, their role extends beyond mere execution. Middle managers are also responsible for translating the organization's strategic goals into actionable plans, motivating and guiding their teams, and acting as intermediaries between upper management and employees.

In essence, middle managers are the organizational glue that holds everything together. They ensure that the company's vision is realized on the ground, adapting strategies to fit the realities of the workplace. This requires a deep understanding of both the organization's objectives and the capabilities and challenges faced by their teams.

Exerting Influence and Driving Change

One of the most significant ways middle managers contribute to organizational success is through their ability to exert influence. Unlike top executives, middle managers often don't have the formal authority to make sweeping changes. However, they can still drive change by leveraging their relationships, communication skills, and deep understanding of their teams and the organization.

Influencing Upward and Downward

Middle managers are uniquely positioned to influence both their superiors and subordinates. They can advocate for their team's needs, provide valuable insights from the frontline, and offer feedback on the feasibility of strategic initiatives. This upward influence is critical for ensuring that senior leaders make informed decisions that consider the realities of day-to-day operations.

At the same time, middle managers can influence their teams by clearly communicating the organization's vision, setting expectations, and motivating employees to achieve their goals. By fostering a positive work environment, providing support, and recognizing achievements, middle managers can drive high performance and ensure that their teams are aligned with the organization's objectives.

Case Study: IBM's Transformation

A notable example of middle management driving change is IBM's transformation in the 1990s. When Louis V. Gerstner Jr. took over as CEO, he initiated a company-wide shift from a hardware-centric business model to one focused on services and software. While this strategic vision came from the top, it was middle managers who played a crucial role in executing the change.

Middle managers at IBM were responsible for implementing new processes, retraining staff, and ensuring that the company's culture evolved to support the new direction. They worked closely with their teams to overcome resistance to change, align employees with the new vision, and drive the company toward its strategic goals. Without the active participation and influence of middle managers, IBM's transformation would have been far more difficult to achieve.

Driving Innovation and Adaptation

Middle managers are also instrumental in fostering innovation and helping organizations adapt to change. Because they are closer to the day-to-day operations, middle managers often have a better understanding of where improvements can be made, what challenges need to be addressed, and what new opportunities might be explored.

By encouraging creativity and providing their teams with the autonomy to experiment, middle managers can drive innovation from the ground up. This bottom-up approach to innovation ensures that ideas are practical and relevant to the organization's needs, increasing the likelihood of successful implementation.

Example: Toyota's Kaizen Approach

Toyota's commitment to continuous improvement, known as Kaizen, is a prime example of how middle managers can drive innovation. At Toyota, middle managers are empowered to identify inefficiencies and work with their teams to develop solutions. This approach has led to numerous innovations in manufacturing processes, improving quality, reducing costs, and enhancing overall productivity.

The success of Kaizen at Toyota is largely due to the active role that middle managers play in fostering a culture of continuous improvement. By encouraging their teams to regularly suggest and implement small changes, middle managers have helped Toyota maintain its competitive edge in the automotive industry.

Contributing to Organizational Success

Middle managers contribute to organizational success in several key ways:

1. Enhancing Communication and Collaboration

Effective communication is critical to any organization's success, and middle managers are often at the heart of this process. They ensure that information flows smoothly between different levels of the organization, helping to prevent misunderstandings and ensuring that everyone is on the same page.

Middle managers also play a key role in fostering collaboration across departments. By facilitating communication and coordinating efforts between different teams, middle managers can help break down silos and ensure that the organization works together toward common goals.

2. Managing Change and Uncertainty

Organizations are constantly facing change, whether it's due to market shifts, technological advancements, or internal restructuring. Middle managers are often on the front lines of managing these changes, helping their teams navigate uncertainty and ensuring that transitions are as smooth as possible.

For example, during mergers or acquisitions, middle managers are critical in maintaining morale, managing expectations, and ensuring that employees remain focused on their work. By providing support and guidance, middle managers can help their teams adapt to new realities and continue to perform at a high level.

3. Developing and Retaining Talent

Middle managers are directly responsible for the development and retention of talent within their teams. By providing regular feedback, identifying opportunities for growth, and supporting employees' professional development, middle managers can help build a strong and capable workforce.

Moreover, middle managers who create a positive and supportive work environment are more likely to retain their top performers. In today's competitive job market, retaining talent is critical to an organization's long-term success, and middle managers play a crucial role in this effort.

Case Study: Google's Project Oxygen

Google's Project Oxygen is an excellent example of how middle managers can contribute to talent development and retention. The project, which began in 2008, aimed to identify what makes a great manager at Google. The findings revealed that middle managers who provided clear guidance, supported career development, and fostered a collaborative environment were key to employee satisfaction and retention.

As a result, Google invested in training programs to help middle managers develop these skills, leading to improved team performance and higher employee retention rates. This case illustrates the significant impact that middle managers can have on an organization's success by focusing on talent development.

CREATING STRATEGIC IMPACT WITHOUT AUTHORITY

In the complex and interconnected world of business, the ability to create strategic impact without formal authority is a vital skill. As a business strategist, understanding how to leverage professional relationships can provide you with the influence needed to drive initiatives, shape decisions, and achieve organizational goals. This approach involves building strong networks, forming alliances, and using interpersonal connections to navigate the decision-making processes. Here's how you can do it.

LEVERAGING RELATIONSHIPS FOR SUCCESS

Professional relationships are the backbone of business success. They involve connections with colleagues, superiors, peers, clients, and other stakeholders who can influence or be influenced by your actions. These relationships are built on trust, mutual respect, and the exchange of value. When cultivated correctly, they can become powerful tools for achieving strategic objectives, especially when you do not have formal authority.

Without a formal title that grants you decision-making power, your ability to influence outcomes depends largely on how well you can manage and leverage these relationships. The key lies in understanding that influence in a business context often comes not from authority, but from the strength and depth of your relationships.

Strategies for Leveraging Professional Relationships

1. Building a Strong Network

Your professional network is your most valuable asset when it comes to exerting influence without formal authority. A strong network provides you with access to information, resources, and allies who can help you achieve your goals.

Cultivating Connections: Start by identifying key individuals within and outside your organization who can impact your objectives. These could include colleagues in different departments, managers, industry experts, or even clients. Focus on building genuine relationships with these individuals by showing interest in their work, offering your help when needed, and consistently staying in touch.

For instance, if you're working on a new project that requires support from the IT department, establish a relationship with the IT manager early on. Regularly communicate with them about the project's progress, seek their input, and appreciate their contributions. This approach not only builds rapport but also positions you as someone who values collaboration.

Expanding Your Network: Attend industry conferences, workshops, and seminars to meet new people and expand your network. Engage in conversations, exchange contact information, and follow up afterward to keep the connection alive. Networking events provide an excellent opportunity to meet potential allies who can support your initiatives.

Leverage social media platforms like LinkedIn to connect with professionals in your field. Join industry-specific groups, participate in discussions, and share valuable content. Online networking can significantly expand your reach and influence.

Case Study: Consider the example of a mid-level marketing manager at a large corporation. Without formal authority, she successfully launched a cross-departmental marketing campaign by leveraging her network. She had previously built strong relationships with the heads of sales, product development, and customer service by collaborating on smaller projects and regularly communicating with them. When it was time to launch the campaign, she used these relationships to gain their support, ensuring a seamless and successful rollout.

2. Building Alliances and Partnerships

Forming alliances within your organization is crucial for creating strategic impact. An alliance is a mutually beneficial relationship where both parties work together to achieve shared goals. By aligning your objectives with those of others, you can pool resources, share information, and amplify your influence.

Identifying Potential Allies: Look for colleagues or departments that share similar goals or face common challenges. These individuals are more likely to support your initiatives because they see the value in collaboration. For example, if you're in charge of improving customer satisfaction, the customer service department would be a natural ally. Their goals align with yours, and together, you can work on initiatives that benefit both teams.

Developing Partnerships: Once you've identified potential allies, focus on building partnerships based on trust and mutual benefit. Start by discussing your goals and how they align with theirs. Clearly outline how working together can help both parties achieve their objectives. Regularly communicate with your partners, involve them in decision-making, and ensure that they feel valued and respected.

Example: A project manager in a tech company once faced significant resistance from the engineering team when trying to implement a new project management tool. Instead of forcing the tool on them, he identified a key engineer who was open to new ideas and formed an alliance. By working closely with this engineer, understanding the team's concerns, and addressing them collaboratively, the project manager gained the support of the entire engineering team, successfully implementing the tool across the department.

3. Influencing Decision-Making Processes

Influencing decision-making without formal authority requires a combination of strategic communication, credibility, and the ability to present compelling arguments. Your goal is to shape the decisions being made by those who do have formal authority.

Building Credibility: Credibility is the foundation of influence. To build credibility, consistently demonstrate your expertise, reliability, and integrity. Deliver on your promises, provide accurate and insightful information, and be transparent in your dealings. The more credible you are, the more likely others are to listen to and consider your input.

Effective Communication: Clear and persuasive communication is essential for influencing decisions. Tailor your message to your audience, focusing on their needs, concerns, and priorities. Use data, evidence, and logical arguments to support your case, but also appeal to emotions when appropriate.

For example, if you're trying to convince senior management to invest in a new initiative, present a well-researched business case that highlights the potential return on investment, aligns with the company's strategic goals, and addresses any potential risks. Additionally, share success stories or testimonials from similar projects that evoke a positive emotional response.

Navigating Organizational Politics: Understanding the political landscape of your organization is crucial for influencing decisions. Identify the key decision-makers and understand their motivations, priorities, and concerns. Use this knowledge to frame your arguments in a way that resonates with them.

For instance, if you know that a particular executive is risk-averse, emphasize the risk mitigation strategies you've put in place for your proposal. If another executive values innovation, highlight how your initiative aligns with the company's innovation goals.

Case Study: A business analyst in a financial services firm wanted to introduce a new data analytics tool that would streamline operations and improve decision-making. However, the executive team was hesitant to invest in new technology. The analyst leveraged his credibility by showcasing his past successes and providing a detailed analysis of the potential benefits. He also formed alliances with department heads who would directly benefit from the tool and had them advocate for the proposal during meetings. By strategically influencing key stakeholders, the analyst successfully gained approval for the tool's implementation.

Practical Tips for Leveraging Professional Relationships

1. Be Proactive in Relationship Building: Don't wait for opportunities to arise actively seek out connections and build relationships with key individuals in your organization. Regularly engage with your network, even when you don't need immediate support. This proactive approach ensures that your relationships are strong and ready to be leveraged when necessary.

2. Offer Value before Seeking Favors: One of the most effective ways to build strong professional relationships is by offering value before seeking anything in return. Share your expertise, provide support, or help solve a problem for your colleagues. By contributing to their success, you build goodwill and establish a foundation for future collaboration.

3. Maintain Regular Communication: Keep your network active by maintaining regular communication. This doesn't mean you need to constantly check in with everyone, but rather stay in touch through periodic updates, informal meetings, or shared professional interests. Regular communication keeps you top of mind and ensures that your relationships remain strong.

4. Show Genuine Interest in Others: Take the time to understand the goals, challenges, and aspirations of the people in your network. Showing genuine interest in others' work and well-being builds trust and strengthens your relationships. When people feel that you care about their success, they are more likely to support you in return.

5. Be Transparent and Authentic: Authenticity is key to building trust in professional relationships. Be honest about your intentions, goals, and limitations. If you need support, clearly communicate why it's important and how it aligns with the other person's interests. Avoid hidden agendas or manipulation, as these can damage your credibility and relationships.

6. Practice Active Listening: Active listening is a powerful tool for building rapport and understanding the needs of others. When engaging with your network, listen more than you speak. Pay attention to verbal and non-verbal cues, ask questions, and acknowledge their perspectives. Active listening shows that you value their input and are committed to mutual success.

7. Recognize and Celebrate Contributions: When others support your initiatives or contribute to your success, recognize their efforts and celebrate their contributions. Publicly acknowledging their role not only strengthens your relationship but also encourages continued collaboration in the future.

Long-Term Relationship Management

Building and leveraging professional relationships is not a one-time effort; it requires ongoing maintenance and attention. To ensure your network remains a valuable asset, focus on long-term relationship management.

1. Regularly Assess Your Network: Periodically review your professional network to ensure it aligns with your current goals and needs. Identify any gaps or areas for improvement, such as relationships that need strengthening or new connections that should be made. A well-maintained network evolves with your career, providing you with the support and resources you need at every stage.

2. Stay Relevant and Informed: To maintain influence, stay informed about industry trends, organizational changes, and the goals of key stakeholders. Regularly update your knowledge and skills to remain a valuable resource to your network. Staying relevant ensures that your input is sought after and your relationships remain strong.

3. Provide Ongoing Support: Continue to offer support and value to your network, even when you don't need immediate assistance. By consistently contributing to others' success, you reinforce the reciprocity that underpins strong professional relationships. This ongoing support also strengthens your reputation as a reliable and valuable ally.

Leveraging Professional Relationships for Strategic Impact without Formal Authority

In today's business environment, the ability to create strategic impact without holding formal authority is crucial. For those who find themselves in roles where they don't have direct decision-making power, leveraging professional relationships can be a powerful way to influence outcomes and drive change. As a business strategist, understanding how to network, build alliances, and influence decision-making processes through interpersonal connections can enable you to make a significant impact within your organization. This section will outline strategies for leveraging professional relationships effectively, offering practical insights into how you can build a robust network, forge alliances, and strategically influence decisions.

Understanding the Importance of Professional Relationships

Professional relationships are the bedrock of effective business strategy. They extend beyond mere acquaintances and involve building trust, mutual respect, and a shared understanding of goals. In the absence of formal authority, these relationships become the primary channel through which influence is exerted and strategic impact is made. Strong professional relationships allow you to navigate the complexities of an organization, gaining the support and cooperation needed to achieve your objectives.

The power of professional relationships lies in their ability to open doors, provide access to resources, and facilitate collaboration. When cultivated with care and intention, these relationships can help you overcome barriers, mobilize support for your initiatives, and influence key decision-makers.

Building a Strong Network

Your network is your most valuable asset in leveraging professional relationships. A strong, diverse network gives you access to a wide range of perspectives, resources, and opportunities. It also enhances your visibility within the organization, making it easier to exert influence.

Developing Meaningful Connections:

To build a strong network, start by identifying key individuals within and outside your organization who can impact your goals. This might include colleagues in other departments, industry peers, clients, or even competitors. Focus on building genuine relationships by showing interest in their work, offering support, and maintaining regular communication.

For example, if you're working on a cross-functional project, take the time to get to know the team members from different departments. Engage with them beyond the project scope—understand their challenges, share insights, and offer help where possible. This approach not only builds rapport but also positions you as a collaborator who values teamwork and mutual success.

Expanding Your Reach:

Attend industry conferences, seminars, and networking events to meet new people and expand your network. These events provide an excellent platform to connect with professionals who share your interests and goals. Engaging in discussions, exchanging ideas, and following up after the event can help you build lasting relationships that extend beyond the initial meeting.

Online platforms like LinkedIn are also valuable tools for expanding your network. Join industry groups, participate in discussions, and share content that reflects your expertise. This not only increases your visibility but also helps you connect with like-minded professionals who can become valuable allies.

Case Study: Building a Network to Drive Innovation

Consider the example of a mid-level manager in a large corporation who was tasked with driving innovation within the company. Without formal authority to enforce changes, she relied on her network to gather support. By cultivating relationships with colleagues in R&D, marketing, and finance, she created a cross-departmental team that collaborated on innovative projects. Her strong network allowed her to gather diverse perspectives, access necessary resources, and ultimately lead successful innovation initiatives within the company.

Forging Strategic Alliances

Building alliances within your organization is a critical strategy for leveraging professional relationships. An alliance is a partnership where both parties work together to achieve shared goals. When you align your objectives with those of others, you can pool resources, share information, and amplify your influence.

Identifying Potential Allies:

Start by identifying colleagues or departments whose goals align with yours. These individuals are more likely to support your initiatives because they see the mutual benefits of collaboration. For example, if your goal is to improve customer satisfaction, align with the customer service department. Their objectives likely overlap with yours, making those natural allies in your efforts.

Developing Collaborative Partnerships:

Once you've identified potential allies, focus on building partnerships based on trust and mutual respect. Begin by discussing your goals and how they align with theirs. Clearly outline the benefits of working together and involve them in the decision-making process. Regular communication and shared successes are key to maintaining strong alliances.

Example: Partnering for Success

A project manager in a tech company faced resistance from the engineering team when trying to implement a new project management tool. Recognizing the need for collaboration, she identified a key engineer who was open to new ideas. By forming a partnership, they addressed the team's concerns together, ultimately gaining the support needed to implement the tool successfully. This example highlights the power of alliances in overcoming resistance and driving change within an organization.

Influencing Decision-Making Processes

Influencing decision-making without formal authority requires strategic communication, credibility, and the ability to present compelling arguments. Your goal is to shape the decisions being made by those who do have formal authority.

Building Credibility:

Credibility is the foundation of influence. To build credibility, consistently demonstrate your expertise, reliability, and integrity. Deliver on your promises, provide accurate and insightful information, and be transparent in your dealings. The more credible you are, the more likely others are to listen to and consider your input.

Effective Communication:

Clear and persuasive communication is essential for influencing decisions. Tailor your message to your audience, focusing on their needs, concerns, and priorities. Use data, evidence, and logical arguments to support your case, but also appeal to emotions when appropriate.

For instance, if you're trying to convince senior management to invest in a new initiative, present a well-researched business case that highlights the potential return on investment, aligns with the company's strategic goals, and addresses any potential risks. Additionally, share success stories or testimonials from similar projects that evoke a positive emotional response.

Navigating Organizational Politics:

Understanding the political landscape of your organization is crucial for influencing decisions. Identify the key decision-makers and understand their motivations, priorities, and concerns. Use this knowledge to frame your arguments in a way that resonates with them.

For example, if you know that a particular executive is risk-averse, emphasize the risk mitigation strategies you've put in place for your proposal. If another executive values innovation, highlight how your initiative aligns with the company's innovation goals.

Case Study: Strategic Influence in Decision-Making

A business analyst in a financial services firm wanted to introduce a new data analytics tool that would streamline operations and improve decision-making. However, the executive team was hesitant to invest in new technology. The analyst leveraged his credibility by showcasing his past successes and providing a detailed analysis of the potential benefits. He also formed alliances with department heads who would directly benefit from the tool and had them advocate for the proposal during meetings. By strategically influencing key stakeholders, the analyst successfully gained approval for the tool's implementation.

Building Long-Term Relationships

Building and leveraging professional relationships is not a one-time effort; it requires ongoing maintenance and attention. To ensure your network remains a valuable asset, focus on long-term relationship management.

Regularly Assess Your Network:

Periodically review your professional network to ensure it aligns with your current goals and needs. Identify any gaps or areas for improvement, such as relationships that need strengthening or new connections that should be made. A well-maintained network evolves with your career, providing you with the support and resources you need at every stage.

Stay Relevant and Informed:

To maintain influence, stay informed about industry trends, organizational changes, and the goals of key stakeholders. Regularly update your knowledge and skills to remain a valuable resource to your network. Staying relevant ensures that your input is sought after and your relationships remain strong.

Provide Ongoing Support:

Continue to offer support and value to your network, even when you don't need immediate assistance. By consistently contributing to others' success, you reinforce the reciprocity that underpins strong professional relationships. This ongoing support also strengthens your reputation as a reliable and valuable ally.

Tips for Successful Relationship Management

1. Be Proactive in Building Relationships: Don't wait for opportunities to arise—actively seek out connections and build relationships with key individuals in your organization. Regularly engage with your network, even when you don't need immediate support. This proactive approach ensures that your relationships are strong and ready to be leveraged when necessary.

2. Offer Value before Seeking Favors: One of the most effective ways to build strong professional relationships is by offering value before seeking anything in return. Share your expertise, provide support, or help solve a problem for your colleagues. By contributing to their success, you build goodwill and establish a foundation for future collaboration.

3. Maintain Regular Communication: Keep your network active by maintaining regular communication. This doesn't mean you need to constantly check in with everyone, but rather stay in touch through periodic updates, informal meetings, or shared professional interests. Regular communication keeps you top of mind and ensures that your relationships remain strong.

4. Show Genuine Interest in Others: Take the time to understand the goals, challenges, and aspirations of the people in your network. Showing genuine interest in others' work and well-being builds trust and strengthens your relationships. When people feel that you care about their success, they are more likely to support you in return.

5. Be Transparent and Authentic: Authenticity is key to building trust in professional relationships. Be honest about your intentions, goals, and limitations. If you need support, clearly communicate why it's important and how it aligns with the other person's interests. Avoid hidden agendas or manipulation, as these can damage your credibility and relationships.

6. Practice Active Listening: Active listening is a powerful tool for building rapport and understanding the needs of others. When engaging with your network, listen more than you speak. Pay attention to verbal and non-verbal cues, ask questions, and acknowledge their perspectives. Active listening shows that you value their input and are committed to mutual success.

7. Recognize and Celebrate Contributions: When others support Professional relationships are crucial for creating strategic impact without formal authority. By building a strong network, forming strategic alliances, and effectively influencing decision-making processes, you can drive change and achieve significant outcomes in your organization. This process involves understanding the power of professional relationships, cultivating connections, developing partnerships, and navigating organizational politics with credibility and effective communication. Long-term relationship management is essential to maintaining influence and ensuring ongoing success.

For a detailed strategy, I'd recommend revisiting and reworking the content I provided to suit your specific needs. If you need further refinements or specific sections reworked to better fit your vision, I'm here to help!

UNDERSTANDING ORGANIZATIONAL DYNAMICS

Understanding organizational dynamics is a critical skill for any leader, particularly for those who hold positions without formal authority. Non-title leaders, or those who lead without a formal managerial or executive title, often rely on their ability to navigate the intricate web of relationships, power structures, company culture, and informal networks within their organization to drive results and influence outcomes. As an organizational development expert, I will explore why understanding these dynamics is essential and how it can empower non-title leaders to excel in their roles.

The Importance of Organizational Dynamics

Organizational dynamics refer to the patterns of interaction, behavior, and relationships within an organization. These dynamics are shaped by various factors, including power structures, company culture, and informal networks. For non-title leaders, who lack the formal authority that comes with a title, the ability to understand and navigate these dynamics is crucial to effectively leading and influencing others.

Power Structures: Navigating Authority and Influence

Power structures within an organization define who holds decision-making authority and how that authority is exercised. While formal power is typically associated with those in leadership positions, there are also informal power structures at play. These informal power structures can be just as influential, if not more so, than formal hierarchies.

For non-title leaders, understanding the power dynamics within their organization is essential. By recognizing who holds formal authority and who wields informal influence, they can identify key stakeholders, allies, and potential obstacles. This awareness allows them to tailor their approach to decision-making processes and to seek support from those who have the power to effect change.

Example: Consider a project coordinator in a large corporation who does not have formal authority over the team members involved in a project. However, by understanding the power dynamics, the coordinator identifies that the head of another department holds significant informal influence despite not being directly involved in the project. By building a relationship with this influential individual, the coordinator can gain their support, which in turn can help sway other team members and senior management in favor of the project's objectives.

Company Culture: Aligning with Organizational Values and Norms

Company culture encompasses the shared values, beliefs, and behaviors that characterize an organization. It influences how employees interact, make decisions, and approach their work. For non-title leaders, aligning their actions and strategies with the prevailing company culture is vital to gaining acceptance and support from colleagues and superiors.

Understanding company culture involves recognizing the unwritten rules and norms that guide behavior within the organization. Non-title leaders who are attuned to these cultural cues can effectively navigate the organization's social landscape, ensuring that their initiatives are perceived as consistent with the company's values.

Example: A non-title leader in a tech startup may recognize that the company culture prioritizes innovation and risk-taking. To drive a new initiative, they might frame their proposal in terms of how it aligns with the company's innovative spirit, emphasizing the potential for the initiative to disrupt the market and lead to significant competitive advantages. By doing so, they increase the likelihood of gaining buy-in from other employees and leadership.

Informal Networks: Leveraging Relationships for Influence

Informal networks refer to the relationships and connections between individuals within an organization that are not defined by the formal organizational chart. These networks often play a crucial role in how work gets done, as they facilitate the flow of information, resources, and support.

For non-title leaders, informal networks are a powerful tool for exerting influence. By cultivating relationships within these networks, they can build alliances, gain access to valuable information, and mobilize support for their initiatives. Understanding the structure and dynamics of informal networks enables non-title leaders to identify key influencers and opinion leaders who can help them achieve their goals.

Example: A non-title leader in a healthcare organization might recognize that the informal network of nurses holds significant sway over the implementation of new patient care protocols. By engaging with and gaining the trust of these nurses, the leader can facilitate the adoption of new protocols, even without formal authority. The support of the informal network ensures that the initiative is embraced and executed effectively across the organization.

Enhancing Leadership through Awareness of Organizational Dynamics

Awareness of organizational dynamics enhances a leader's ability to influence and drive results in several key ways. By understanding power structures, company culture, and informal networks, non-title leaders can develop strategies that align with the organization's dynamics, build credibility, and effectively communicate their vision.

1. Building Credibility and Trust

One of the most significant benefits of understanding organizational dynamics is the ability to build credibility and trust. Non-title leaders often rely on their reputation and relationships to influence others. By demonstrating a deep understanding of the organization's dynamics, they can establish themselves as knowledgeable and trustworthy.

For instance, when a non-title leader accurately anticipates the concerns and motivations of key stakeholders, they can address these issues proactively, earning the respect and confidence of their colleagues. This credibility becomes a foundation for effective leadership, allowing the non-title leader to influence decisions and drive change.

2. Strategic Communication and Persuasion

Effective communication is critical for any leader, but it is especially important for non-title leaders who must rely on persuasion rather than authority. Understanding organizational dynamics allows these leaders to tailor their communication strategies to resonate with their audience.

For example, by recognizing the dominant values within the company culture, a non-title leader can frame their messages in a way that aligns with those values. This approach makes their proposals more compelling and increases the likelihood of gaining support. Additionally, by identifying key influencers within informal networks, non-title leaders can strategically target their communication efforts to ensure that their messages are disseminated effectively throughout the organization.

3. Facilitating Collaboration and Cooperation

Collaboration is essential for achieving organizational goals, and non-title leaders play a crucial role in fostering cooperation among team members and departments. By understanding the dynamics of power structures and informal networks, these leaders can identify potential collaborators and build cross-functional teams that leverage diverse skills and perspectives.

For instance, a non-title leader who understands the informal network within their organization can bring together individuals from different departments who might not typically collaborate but who share a common interest or expertise. This approach can lead to more innovative solutions and a greater sense of ownership and commitment among team members.

4. Navigating Organizational Change

Change is a constant in today's business environment, and non-title leaders are often at the forefront of driving and managing change within their organizations. Understanding organizational dynamics is crucial for navigating the complexities of change management.

Non-title leaders who are aware of the power structures and informal networks within their organization can anticipate resistance to change and develop strategies to address it. They can identify potential change champions within the organization and leverage their influence to build momentum for the change initiative. Additionally, by aligning their change efforts with the company culture, non-title leaders can ensure that their initiatives are perceived as credible and legitimate, increasing the likelihood of successful implementation.

5. Conflict Resolution and Problem-Solving

Conflict is an inevitable part of organizational life, and non-title leaders often find themselves in the role of mediator or problem-solver. Understanding organizational dynamics enables these leaders to navigate conflicts effectively by identifying the underlying power structures, cultural norms, and informal relationships that contribute to the conflict.

For example, a non-title leader who is aware of the informal network of alliances within a team can use this knowledge to mediate conflicts by facilitating dialogue between key influencers. By addressing the concerns of these influencers and seeking their input in the resolution process, the leader can foster a more collaborative and constructive approach to conflict resolution.

MASTERING COMMUNICATION: THE KEY TO INFLUENCE

In leadership, the ability to influence without formal authority is a crucial skill. Persuasive communication plays a central role in this process, enabling leaders to inspire, motivate, and guide others toward a shared vision. As a communications specialist, this guide will explore the key techniques leaders can use to communicate persuasively, focusing on rhetoric, body language, and emotional appeal. These techniques are essential for any leader looking to exert influence, build trust, and drive change within an organization.

PERSUASIVE COMMUNICATION TECHNIQUES

Persuasion is the art of convincing others to embrace your ideas, beliefs, or actions. In leadership, it is particularly important when you don't have formal authority or when you need to gain buy-in from stakeholders, peers, or team members. Persuasive communication goes beyond merely presenting facts; it involves connecting with your audience on an emotional and psychological level, understanding their needs and motivations, and using various techniques to align their perspectives with yours.

Rhetoric: The Art of Effective Speaking and Writing

Rhetoric is the art of using language effectively and persuasively. It is a powerful tool for leaders, enabling them to articulate their vision, influence opinions, and inspire action. Aristotle, the ancient Greek philosopher, identified three key components of rhetoric: ethos (credibility), pathos (emotional appeal), and logos (logical reasoning). Understanding and applying these components can significantly enhance a leader's ability to communicate persuasively.

1. Ethos: Establishing Credibility

Ethos refers to the credibility or ethical appeal of the speaker. For a leader to be persuasive, they must first establish themselves as trustworthy and knowledgeable. This credibility can be built through expertise, experience, and demonstrating integrity.

Building Credibility:

Expertise: Demonstrate your knowledge and experience in the subject matter. This can be done through sharing your qualifications, past successes, or relevant experiences.

Integrity: Consistently act with honesty and transparency. Leaders who are perceived as fair and ethical are more likely to gain the trust and respect of their audience.

Connection: Show that you understand and care about the concerns and values of your audience. This builds a rapport and makes your message more relatable.

Example of Ethos in Leadership: Consider a project manager who needs to convince the team to adopt a new workflow. By sharing her past success in implementing similar workflows and showing a deep understanding of the team's current challenges, she builds credibility. Her team is more likely to trust her judgment and follow her lead because they perceive her as an expert who has their best interests at heart.

2. Pathos: Engaging Emotionally

Pathos is the emotional appeal used to persuade an audience. Emotions play a significant role in decision-making, often influencing people more than logic alone. Leaders who can tap into the emotions of their audience can create a stronger connection and motivate action.

Using Emotional Appeal:

Storytelling: Share stories that evoke emotions, whether it's inspiration, empathy, or a sense of urgency. Stories make your message more memorable and relatable.

Expressing Passion: Show genuine enthusiasm and passion for your message. Your emotional investment can be contagious, encouraging others to feel similarly.

Addressing Fears and Desires: Understand the fears, hopes, and desires of your audience, and address them directly. Show how your message aligns with their emotional needs.

Example of Pathos in Leadership: A CEO addressing employees during a challenging time might share a personal story of overcoming adversity. By connecting emotionally with the team and expressing optimism about the future, the CEO can inspire confidence and resilience among employees, motivating them to stay committed and focused.

3. Logos: Logical Reasoning

Logos refers to the logical appeal of your argument. This involves using facts, data, and logical reasoning to support your message. While emotions are powerful, logic is necessary to build a strong and convincing argument that can withstand scrutiny.

Building a Logical Argument:

Data and Evidence: Use statistics, research findings, and factual information to support your claims. This strengthens your argument and makes it more credible.

Clear Structure: Present your ideas in a clear, organized manner. This helps your audience follow your reasoning and understand the connections between your points.

Addressing Counterarguments: Anticipate potential objections and address them in your argument. This shows that you've considered different perspectives and strengthens your position.

Example of Logos in Leadership: A sales manager trying to persuade the executive team to invest in new customer relationship management (CRM) software might present data showing how the software has increased sales efficiency in similar companies. By providing a clear cost-benefit analysis, the manager uses logical reasoning to build a compelling case for the investment.

Body Language: Communicating Beyond Words

Body language is a critical aspect of communication that often speaks louder than words. It includes facial expressions, gestures, posture, eye contact, and other non-verbal cues. Effective leaders use body language to reinforce their message, convey confidence, and build rapport with their audience.

1. Posture and Presence

Your posture and overall physical presence can convey confidence and authority or, conversely, uncertainty and insecurity. A strong, upright posture with open gestures communicates confidence, openness, and readiness to engage.

Tips for Effective Posture:

Stand Tall: Keep your back straight and shoulders relaxed. This posture exudes confidence and helps you command attention.

Open Gestures: Use open hand gestures to emphasize your points and convey openness and honesty. Avoid crossing your arms, as this can signal defensiveness.

Occupy Space: Take up space with your posture, whether standing or sitting. This conveys authority and self-assurance.

Example of Posture in Leadership: A team leader presenting a new strategy to the board might stand tall, with shoulders back and hands open, to project confidence and assertiveness. This posture not only reinforces the leader's message but also instills confidence in the board members regarding the leader's ability to execute the strategy.

2. Eye Contact

Eye contact is one of the most powerful tools in persuasive communication. It helps to build trust, convey sincerity, and engage your audience. Maintaining eye contact shows that you are confident, attentive, and focused on the conversation.

Using Eye Contact Effectively:

Engage with the Audience: Maintain eye contact with different members of your audience, not just one person. This makes everyone feel included and engaged.

Balanced Contact: Avoid staring too intensely, as this can be intimidating. Instead, aim for a natural rhythm of eye contact, breaking it occasionally to avoid discomfort.

Show Empathy: Use soft, empathetic eye contact when discussing sensitive or emotional topics. This helps convey understanding and compassion.

Example of Eye Contact in Leadership: During a difficult conversation about performance, a manager who maintains steady, empathetic eye contact with the employee can create a sense of trust and openness. The employee is more likely to feel heard and respected, making the conversation more productive and positive.

3. Facial Expressions and Gestures

Facial expressions and gestures add nuance and emphasis to your verbal communication. They can express enthusiasm, concern, approval, or disapproval, and help convey the emotional tone of your message.

Using Facial Expressions and Gestures:

Smile: A genuine smile can create a positive atmosphere, making your audience more receptive to your message.

Nod for Emphasis: Nodding slightly while speaking can reinforce your points and encourage agreement from your audience.

Controlled Expressions: Be mindful of your facial expressions, ensuring they align with your message. Avoid expressions that might convey unintended emotions, such as frustration or indifference.

Example of Facial Expressions in Leadership: A supervisor delivering praise to a team might use a warm smile and nodding to convey genuine appreciation. This non-verbal communication reinforces the verbal praise, making it more impactful and encouraging for the team.

Emotional Appeal: Connecting on a Deeper Level

Emotional appeal, or pathos, is about connecting with your audience's emotions to persuade them. It involves understanding and addressing the emotional needs and desires of your audience. Leaders who can effectively appeal to emotions can motivate, inspire, and drive action.

1. Storytelling

Storytelling is a powerful way to connect emotionally with your audience. Stories are memorable, relatable, and can evoke strong emotions. They help illustrate your points in a way that resonates on a personal level.

Crafting Compelling Stories:

Personal Experiences: Share personal experiences that are relevant to your message. This adds authenticity and helps your audience relate to you.

Vivid Imagery: Use descriptive language to paint a vivid picture, making the story more engaging and impactful.

Clear Moral: Ensure your story has a clear takeaway or moral that aligns with your message.

Example of Storytelling in Leadership: A CEO trying to rally the company around a new vision might share a personal story of overcoming a significant challenge. By detailing the struggles and ultimate success, the CEO can inspire employees to embrace the new direction with a sense of purpose and determination.

2. Addressing Fears and Desires

People are often motivated by their fears and desires. By addressing these emotions directly, leaders can persuade their audience to take action or change their perspective.

Techniques for Addressing Fears and Desires:

Highlight Benefits: Emphasize how your proposal will meet the desires of your audience, such as increased security, recognition, or success.

Alleviate Fears: Acknowledge the fears or concerns your audience may have and provide reassurance or solutions to mitigate them.

Create Urgency: Highlight the consequences of inaction, creating a sense of urgency that motivates your audience to act.

Example of Addressing Fears and Desires in Leadership: A marketing director proposing

In leadership, especially when you lack formal authority, persuasive communication is essential to influencing others and driving change. This guide explores key techniques that can help leaders communicate effectively and persuasively, focusing on rhetoric, body language, and emotional appeal. Each technique is explained in detail, with real-world examples to illustrate how these strategies can be applied in leadership scenarios.

The Power of Persuasion in Leadership

Persuasion in leadership goes beyond simply presenting facts; it involves connecting with your audience on an emotional and psychological level. Whether you're leading a team, influencing stakeholders, or driving change within an organization, the ability to persuade effectively is crucial. Persuasive communication allows leaders to inspire, motivate, and guide others, even without formal authority.

Rhetoric: The Art of Effective Speaking and Writing

Rhetoric, the art of using language effectively, is a powerful tool for leaders. It encompasses the use of ethos (credibility), pathos (emotional appeal), and logos (logical reasoning) to persuade others.

Ethos: Establishing Credibility

Ethos refers to the credibility of the speaker. For leaders to be persuasive, they must establish themselves as trustworthy and knowledgeable. This involves demonstrating expertise, integrity, and a connection with the audience.

Example: A project manager can build credibility by sharing relevant experiences and demonstrating a deep understanding of the team's challenges. This helps the team trust the manager's guidance and follow their lead.

Pathos: Engaging Emotionally

Pathos is the emotional appeal used to persuade an audience. Leaders who tap into the emotions of their audience can create a stronger connection and motivate action.

Example: A CEO might share a personal story of overcoming adversity to inspire employees during challenging times, fostering a sense of resilience and commitment.

Logos: Logical Reasoning

Logos involves using facts, data, and logical reasoning to support your argument. While emotions are powerful, logic is necessary to build a strong and convincing argument.

Example: A sales manager might present data showing the potential return on investment for a new initiative to persuade the executive team to approve it.

Body Language: Communicating Beyond Words

Body language, including facial expressions, gestures, posture, and eye contact, plays a significant role in communication. Effective leaders use body language to reinforce their message and build rapport with their audience.

Posture and Presence

A strong, upright posture with open gestures conveys confidence and openness, making your message more persuasive.

Example: A leader presenting a new strategy might stand tall and use open hand gestures to project confidence and authority.

Eye Contact

Eye contact builds trust, conveys sincerity, and engages your audience. Maintaining eye contact shows that you are confident and focused.

Example: During a performance review, a manager who maintains steady eye contact can create a sense of trust and openness with the employee.

Facial Expressions and Gestures

Facial expressions and gestures add nuance to your communication. A genuine smile or nod can reinforce your message and make it more impactful.

Example: A leader praising a team might use a warm smile and nodding to convey genuine appreciation, making the praise more meaningful.

Emotional Appeal: Connecting on a Deeper Level

Emotional appeal, or pathos, involves connecting with your audience's emotions to persuade them. Leaders who can effectively appeal to emotions can motivate, inspire, and drive action.

Storytelling

Storytelling is a powerful way to connect emotionally with your audience. Stories are memorable and relatable, making your message more impactful.

Example: A leader might share a story of how a previous team overcame a challenge, inspiring the current team to do the same.

Addressing Fears and Desires

People are often motivated by their fears and desires. By addressing these emotions directly, leaders can persuade their audience to take action or change their perspective.

Example: A marketing director proposing a new campaign might highlight the risks of not adapting to market changes, creating a sense of urgency and motivating the team to act.

Putting It All Together: Applying Persuasive Communication Techniques

Effective leaders combine rhetoric, body language, and emotional appeal to communicate persuasively. By understanding and applying these techniques, leaders can influence others and drive change, even without formal authority.

Building Credibility with Ethos

Establishing credibility is the foundation of persuasive communication. Leaders can build credibility by demonstrating expertise, acting with integrity, and connecting with their audience.

Example: A department head who consistently delivers on promises and provides valuable insights during meetings builds a reputation as a credible leader, making it easier to persuade others.

Engaging Emotions with Pathos

Engaging your audience emotionally can make your message more powerful. Leaders can use storytelling, express passion, and address fears and desires to connect with their audience on a deeper level.

Example: A nonprofit leader might share a story about a beneficiary who was positively impacted by the organization's work, evoking empathy and inspiring donors to contribute.

Supporting Arguments with Logos

Logical reasoning is essential for building a strong, persuasive argument. Leaders should use data, evidence, and clear structure to support their messages and anticipate counterarguments.

Example: A financial analyst might use market data to support a recommendation for a new investment strategy, making the argument more convincing to stakeholders.

Reinforcing Messages with Body Language

Body language can reinforce or undermine your verbal communication. Leaders should use confident posture, maintain eye contact, and align facial expressions with their message to enhance their persuasiveness.

Example: A team leader addressing concerns about a project's timeline might use open gestures and maintain eye contact to convey transparency and confidence.

Connecting with Your Audience

Persuasion is most effective when leaders connect with their audience. By understanding the audience's needs, values, and emotions, leaders can tailor their messages to resonate more effectively.

Example: A manager seeking to implement a new process might first listen to employees' concerns and then address those concerns directly, making the employees feel heard and more likely to support the change.

LISTENING AND FEEDBACK LOOPS

Active listening and feedback loops are essential components of effective leadership, especially for those who lack formal authority but still need to influence and guide others. These practices help leaders build trust, improve team dynamics, and enhance their influence, creating an environment where collaboration and open communication thrive. In this section, we will explore the importance of active listening and feedback loops in leadership, providing actionable advice and real-world examples to illustrate how these techniques can be applied successfully.

The Importance of Active Listening in Leadership

Active listening is more than just hearing words; it involves fully engaging with the speaker, understanding their message, and responding thoughtfully. For leaders, especially those without formal authority, active listening is a powerful tool for building trust, fostering open communication, and creating a supportive environment where team members feel valued and heard.

1. Building Trust through Active Listening

Trust is the foundation of any successful relationship, particularly in a leadership context. When leaders actively listen to their team members, they demonstrate that they respect and value their opinions. This builds trust, as team members feel confident that their concerns and ideas will be taken seriously.

Active listening involves paying close attention to the speaker, asking clarifying questions, and providing feedback that shows you understand their perspective. When team members see that their leader genuinely listens to them, they are more likely to trust that leader, even in the absence of formal authority.

Example: Imagine a team member approaches a leader with a concern about a project deadline. Instead of dismissing the concern or offering a quick solution, the leader listens carefully, asks questions to fully understand the issue, and then discusses possible solutions with the team member. By taking the time to listen actively, the leader builds trust, making the team member feel supported and valued.

2. Improving Team Dynamics through Active Listening

Effective team dynamics are crucial for achieving organizational goals. Active listening helps to improve these dynamics by promoting open communication, reducing misunderstandings, and fostering collaboration.

When leaders practice active listening, they create an environment where team members feel comfortable sharing their ideas and concerns. This openness encourages collaboration, as team members are more likely to contribute to discussions and work together to find solutions. Additionally, active listening helps to prevent misunderstandings that can lead to conflict, as leaders can clarify any ambiguities before they escalate.

Example: A team is struggling to meet a tight deadline, and tensions are rising. The leader notices the strain and holds a meeting where they encourage everyone to share their thoughts on the situation. By actively listening to each team member, the leader identifies the root cause of the tension—a lack of clear communication—and takes steps to address it. As a result, the team works more cohesively, improving their overall dynamics and productivity.

3. Enhancing Influence through Active Listening

For leaders without formal authority, influence is often gained through the relationships they build and the respect they earn. Active listening is a key factor in enhancing this influence, as it shows that the leader is approachable, empathetic, and committed to the team's success.

When leaders listen actively, they gain valuable insights into their team members' motivations, concerns, and strengths. This understanding allows them to tailor their leadership approach to meet the needs of the team, which in turn enhances their influence. Team members are more likely to follow a leader who listens to them, understands their perspective, and takes their input into account when making decisions.

Example: A project manager without formal authority needs to secure the cooperation of various departments to complete a cross-functional project. By actively listening to the concerns and priorities of each department head, the manager can address their needs and build a collaborative working relationship. This approach not only enhances the manager's influence but also increases the likelihood of the project's success.

The Role of Feedback Loops in Leadership

Feedback loops are continuous cycles of feedback exchange between leaders and team members. They play a crucial role in leadership by providing opportunities for growth, reinforcing positive behaviors, and ensuring that everyone is aligned with the organization's goals. Effective feedback loops are characterized by regular, constructive communication that is both giving and receiving feedback.

1. Building Trust through Feedback Loops

Just as with active listening, feedback loops are essential for building trust within a team. When leaders provide constructive feedback, they show that they are invested in the development of their team members. Likewise, when leaders actively seek feedback, they demonstrate humility and a willingness to improve, which further builds trust.

Feedback loops create a safe space for open communication, where team members feel confident that their contributions are valued and that they can speak up without fear of negative repercussions. This trust is crucial for leaders without formal authority, as it encourages team members to follow their guidance based on respect and mutual understanding.

Example: A leader conducts regular one-on-one meetings with team members, where they provide constructive feedback on recent work and ask for feedback on their leadership style. This ongoing exchange builds trust, as team members feel that their opinions are valued and that the leader is genuinely committed to their development.

2. Improving Team Dynamics through Feedback Loops

Feedback loops help to maintain healthy team dynamics by ensuring that communication is ongoing, issues are addressed promptly, and everyone remains aligned with the team's objectives. Regular feedback helps to prevent misunderstandings and conflicts from festering, as team members are encouraged to voice their concerns early.

Incorporating feedback loops into the team's regular practices also fosters a culture of continuous improvement. When feedback is viewed as a positive, constructive tool, rather than a punitive measure, team members are more likely to embrace it and use it to enhance their performance.

Example: A leader implements a weekly feedback loop in team meetings, where each member shares what went well during the week and what could be improved. This practice not only surfaces potential issues before they become significant problems but also promotes a culture of continuous learning and improvement, leading to stronger team dynamics.

3. Enhancing Influence through Feedback Loops

For leaders without formal authority, feedback loops are a powerful way to enhance their influence. By consistently providing valuable, constructive feedback, leaders demonstrate their expertise and commitment to the team's success. Additionally, by seeking feedback from others, leaders show that they value input and are open to improving their approach, which can increase their credibility and influence.

Feedback loops also provide leaders with insights into how their actions and decisions are perceived by the team. This knowledge allows leaders to adjust their strategies to better align with the team's needs and expectations, thereby enhancing their influence and effectiveness.

Example: A leader without formal authority leads a team through a complex project. Throughout the project, the leader regularly provides feedback to team members, helping them overcome challenges and improve their performance. At the same time, the leader seeks feedback on how the team feels about the project's progress and their leadership style. This continuous exchange of feedback builds the leader's influence, as the team recognizes their commitment to both individual and collective success.

Actionable Advice for Implementing Active Listening and Feedback Loops

To effectively implement active listening and feedback loops in your leadership approach, consider the following actionable steps:

1. Practice Active Listening Daily

Active listening is a skill that improves with practice. Make a conscious effort to engage in active listening during every interaction with your team. This means giving your full attention to the speaker, avoiding interruptions, and asking clarifying questions to ensure you fully understand their message.

Tips:

Maintain Eye Contact: Show that you are engaged by maintaining eye contact with the speaker.

Avoid Distractions: Put away phones, close laptops, and focus entirely on the conversation.

Paraphrase: Repeat what the speaker has said in your own words to confirm your understanding.

Example: During a team meeting, a leader notices that one member is quieter than usual. The leader asks them for their thoughts on the topic being discussed and listens actively to their response, ensuring that their perspective is heard and considered.

2. Create Regular Feedback Opportunities

Incorporate feedback loops into your regular leadership practices by creating consistent opportunities for feedback exchange. This can be done through one-on-one meetings, team meetings, or anonymous surveys.

Tips:

Schedule Regular Check-Ins: Set aside time for regular feedback sessions, whether weekly, bi-weekly, or monthly.

Encourage Openness: Foster an environment where team members feel comfortable giving and receiving feedback.

Act on Feedback: Show that you value feedback by taking action based on the input you receive.

Example: A leader implements a monthly feedback survey, where team members can anonymously provide feedback on the team's performance and the leader's approach. The leader reviews the feedback and shares key takeaways with the team, along with specific actions they plan to take in response.

3. Use Feedback to Foster Growth

Feedback should be viewed as an opportunity for growth and improvement, rather than as criticism. When providing feedback, focus on constructive, actionable insights that can help team members develop their skills and achieve their goals.

Tips:

Be Specific: Provide specific examples of what the team member did well and what could be improved.

Focus on the Future: Frame feedback in terms of future actions and improvements, rather than dwelling on past mistakes.

Celebrate Successes: Acknowledge and celebrate the team member's successes and improvements over time.

Example: A leader notices that a team member has been struggling with time management. During a feedback session, the leader provides specific examples of where the team member could improve, along with suggestions for time management tools and techniques. The leader also acknowledges the team member's strengths and encourages them to continue developing their skills.

The Power of Active Listening and Feedback Loops in Leadership

Active listening and feedback loops are indispensable tools for leaders, particularly those who lack formal authority. These practices help leaders build trust, improve team dynamics, and enhance their influence by fostering open communication, continuous learning, and a culture of mutual respect. By incorporating active listening and feedback loops into their leadership approach, leaders can create a supportive Active listening and feedback loops are essential components of effective leadership, especially for those who lack formal authority but still need to influence and guide others. These practices help leaders build trust, improve team dynamics, and enhance their influence, creating an environment where collaboration and open communication thrive. In this section, we will explore the importance of active listening and feedback loops in leadership, providing actionable advice and real-world examples to illustrate how these techniques can be applied successfully.

The Importance of Active Listening in Leadership

Active listening is more than just hearing words; it involves fully engaging with the speaker, understanding their message, and responding thoughtfully. For leaders, especially those without formal authority, active listening is a powerful tool for building trust, fostering open communication, and creating a supportive environment where team members feel valued and heard.

Building Trust through Active Listening

Trust is the foundation of any successful relationship, particularly in a leadership context. When leaders actively listen to their team members, they demonstrate that they respect and value their opinions. This builds trust, as team members feel confident that their concerns and ideas will be taken seriously.

Active listening involves paying close attention to the speaker, asking clarifying questions, and providing feedback that shows you understand their perspective. When team members see that their leader genuinely listens to them, they are more likely to trust that leader, even in the absence of formal authority.

Example: Imagine a team member approaches a leader with a concern about a project deadline. Instead of dismissing the concern or offering a quick solution, the leader listens carefully, asks questions to fully understand the issue, and then discusses possible solutions with the team member. By taking the time to listen actively, the leader builds trust, making the team member feel supported and valued.

Improving Team Dynamics through Active Listening

Effective team dynamics are crucial for achieving organizational goals. Active listening helps to improve these dynamics by promoting open communication, reducing misunderstandings, and fostering collaboration.

When leaders practice active listening, they create an environment where team members feel comfortable sharing their ideas and concerns. This openness encourages collaboration, as team members are more likely to contribute to discussions and work together to find solutions. Additionally, active listening helps to prevent misunderstandings that can lead to conflict, as leaders can clarify any ambiguities before they escalate.

Example: A team is struggling to meet a tight deadline, and tensions are rising. The leader notices the strain and holds a meeting where they encourage everyone to share their thoughts on the situation. By actively listening to each team member, the leader identifies the root cause of the tension—a lack of clear communication and takes steps to address it. As a result, the team works more cohesively, improving their overall dynamics and productivity.

Enhancing Influence through Active Listening

For leaders without formal authority, influence is often gained through the relationships they build and the respect they earn. Active listening is a key factor in enhancing this influence, as it shows that the leader is approachable, empathetic, and committed to the team's success.

When leaders listen actively, they gain valuable insights into their team members' motivations, concerns, and strengths. This understanding allows them to tailor their leadership approach to meet the needs of the team, which in turn enhances their influence. Team members are more likely to follow a leader who listens to them, understands their perspective, and takes their input into account when making decisions.

Example: A project manager without formal authority needs to secure the cooperation of various departments to complete a cross-functional project. By actively listening to the concerns and priorities of each department head, the manager can address their needs and build a collaborative working relationship. This approach not only enhances the manager's influence but also increases the likelihood of the project's success.

The Role of Feedback Loops in Leadership

Feedback loops are continuous cycles of feedback exchange between leaders and team members. They play a crucial role in leadership by providing opportunities for growth, reinforcing positive behaviors, and ensuring that everyone is aligned with the organization's goals. Effective feedback loops are characterized by regular, constructive communication that is both giving and receiving feedback.

Building Trust through Feedback Loops

Just as with active listening, feedback loops are essential for building trust within a team. When leaders provide constructive feedback, they show that they are invested in the development of their team members. Likewise, when leaders actively seek feedback, they demonstrate humility and a willingness to improve, which further builds trust.

Feedback loops create a safe space for open communication, where team members feel confident that their contributions are valued and that they can speak up without fear of negative repercussions. This trust is crucial for leaders without formal authority, as it encourages team members to follow their guidance based on respect and mutual understanding.

Example: A leader conducts regular one-on-one meetings with team members, where they provide constructive feedback on recent work and ask for feedback on their leadership style. This ongoing exchange builds trust, as team members feel that their opinions are valued and that the leader is genuinely committed to their development.

Improving Team Dynamics through Feedback Loops

Feedback loops help to maintain healthy team dynamics by ensuring that communication is ongoing, issues are addressed promptly, and everyone remains aligned with the team's objectives. Regular feedback helps to prevent misunderstandings and conflicts from festering, as team members are encouraged to voice their concerns early.

Incorporating feedback loops into the team's regular practices also fosters a culture of continuous improvement. When feedback is viewed as a positive, constructive tool, rather than a punitive measure, team members are more likely to embrace it and use it to enhance their performance.

Example: A leader implements a weekly feedback loop in team meetings, where each member shares what went well during the week and what could be improved. This practice not only surfaces potential issues before they become significant problems but also promotes a culture of continuous learning and improvement, leading to stronger team dynamics.

Enhancing Influence through Feedback Loops

For leaders without formal authority, feedback loops are a powerful way to enhance their influence. By consistently providing valuable, constructive feedback, leaders demonstrate their expertise and commitment to the team's success. Additionally, by seeking feedback from others, leaders show that they value input and are open to improving their approach, which can increase their credibility and influence.

Feedback loops also provide leaders with insights into how their actions and decisions are perceived by the team. This knowledge allows leaders to adjust their strategies to better align with the team's needs and expectations, thereby enhancing their influence and effectiveness.

Example: A leader without formal authority leads a team through a complex project. Throughout the project, the leader regularly provides feedback to team members, helping them overcome challenges and improve their performance. At the same time, the leader seeks feedback on how the team feels about the project's progress and their leadership style. This continuous exchange of feedback builds the leader's influence, as the team recognizes their commitment to both individual and collective success.

PART II: CULTIVATING PERSONAL LEADERSHIP

SELF-LEADERSHIP: THE FIRST STEP TO LEADING OTHERS

As a personal development coach, one of the most crucial aspects of self-leadership I emphasize is the cultivation of self-discipline and motivation. These foundational skills empower individuals to take control of their lives, achieve their goals, and lead others effectively. This guide will provide you with practical exercises, habit-building strategies, and real-world examples to help you develop these essential qualities.

DEVELOPING DISCIPLINE AND SELF-MOTIVATION

Self-discipline is the ability to control your impulses, emotions, and behaviors to achieve long-term goals. It's about making choices that align with your values and objectives, even when they're not the easiest or most immediately gratifying options. Self-discipline enables you to stay focused on your path and resist distractions or temptations that could derail your progress.

Motivation, on the other hand, is the driving force behind your actions. It's what gets you started on a task and keeps you going, even when challenges arise. Motivation can come from internal sources, like personal values and goals (intrinsic motivation), or external sources, like rewards and recognition (extrinsic motivation).

Together, self-discipline and motivation form a powerful duo that fuels self-leadership. While motivation gets you started, self-discipline keeps you on track, ensuring that you follow through on your commitments and achieve your goals.

Developing self-discipline is a gradual process that requires consistent practice. Here are some practical exercises to help you build this crucial skill:

1. Set Clear Goals

Clear, specific goals provide direction and purpose. Without clear goals, it's easy to become distracted or lose focus. Start by defining what you want to achieve, both in the short term and long term. Break down larger goals into smaller, manageable tasks that you can work on consistently.

Exercise:

Write down your top three goals for the next six months. For each goal, list the specific actions you need to take to achieve them.

Break these actions down into daily or weekly tasks and prioritize them based on their importance.

Example: If your goal is to improve your physical fitness, your smaller tasks might include scheduling three weekly workouts, preparing healthy meals in advance, and tracking your progress.

2. Create a Routine

Routines help to automate discipline by turning desired behaviors into habits. When you consistently perform certain actions at the same time each day, they become ingrained in your routine, requiring less mental effort to maintain.

Exercise:

- Identify key areas where you want to improve your discipline (e.g., exercise, work productivity, healthy eating).
- Design a daily routine that incorporates these activities at specific times.
- Commit to following this routine for at least 21 days to help establish new habits.

Example: If you want to become more disciplined in your work, you might set aside the first two hours of each workday for focused, uninterrupted tasks, with a 10-minute break afterward as a reward.

3. Practice Delayed Gratification

Delayed gratification is the ability to resist the temptation of an immediate reward in favor of a larger, long-term benefit. It's a key component of self-discipline and can be developed through practice.

Exercise:

- Identify a habit where you typically seek immediate gratification (e.g., snacking, procrastinating).
- Challenge yourself to delay that gratification by 10 minutes, then gradually increase the delay over time.
- Use this time to focus on the long-term benefits of resisting the temptation.

Example: If you're trying to cut down on unhealthy snacks, delay eating a treat by 10 minutes while you drink a glass of water or distract yourself with another task. Over time, this practice will strengthen your ability to delay gratification in other areas.

4. Use Positive Reinforcement

Positive reinforcement involves rewarding yourself for making disciplined choices. This reinforces the behavior and makes it more likely that you'll repeat it in the future.

Exercise:

- ❖ Set up a reward system for completing your daily or weekly tasks. The rewards can be small, like taking a break or enjoying a favorite activity.
- ❖ Make sure the rewards are aligned with your goals and do not undermine your progress.

Example: If you complete all your planned workouts for the week, reward yourself with a relaxing activity, like watching a movie or taking a long bath. The anticipation of the reward can motivate you to stay disciplined.

Cultivating Motivation: Strategies and Tips

While self-discipline keeps you on track, motivation provides the energy and enthusiasm to pursue your goals. Here's how to cultivate and sustain motivation:

1. Connect with Your 'Why'

Understanding the deeper reasons behind your goals can provide powerful motivation. Reflect on why your goals are important to you and how achieving they will improve your life.

Exercise:

- ❖ Take some time to journal about your goals and why they matter to you. Be honest and detailed in your reflections.
- ❖ Keep this journal entry handy and refer to it whenever you feel your motivation waning.

Example: If your goal is to advance in your career, your 'why' might be to provide a better future for your family or to achieve personal fulfillment. Keeping this purpose in mind can motivate you to push through challenges.

2. Visualize Success

Visualization is a technique where you imagine yourself achieving your goals in vivid detail. This mental imagery can create positive emotions and increase your motivation to take action.

Exercise:

- ❖ Spend a few minutes each day visualizing yourself achieving your goals. Imagine how you'll feel, what you'll see, and what you'll hear.
- ❖ Use all your senses to make the visualization as realistic as possible.

Example: If your goal is to run a marathon, visualize yourself crossing the finish line, feeling strong and accomplished. This positive imagery can help you stay motivated during training.

3. Surround Yourself with Positivity

Your environment and the people you interact with can significantly impact your motivation. Surround yourself with supportive, positive influences that encourage you to stay focused on your goals.

Exercise:

- ❖ Identify any negative influences in your environment (e.g., unsupportive friends, cluttered workspace) and take steps to minimize their impact.
- ❖ Seek out positive influences, such as joining a community of like-minded individuals or following inspiring role models.

Example: If you're trying to eat healthier, surround yourself with friends who share your goals, or join an online group where members share tips and recipes. The support and encouragement you receive can boost your motivation.

4. Break down Goals and Celebrate Milestones

Large goals can sometimes feel overwhelming, leading to a loss of motivation. By breaking them down into smaller, more manageable milestones, you can maintain a sense of progress and achievement.

Exercise:

- Divide your larger goals into smaller milestones with specific deadlines.
- Celebrate each milestone you achieve, no matter how small.

Example: If your goal is to write a book, break it down into milestones like completing the outline, writing each chapter, and editing. Celebrate each milestone with a small reward, like treating yourself to your favorite snack or taking a day off.

Habit-Building Strategies for Long-Term Success

Developing self-discipline and motivation requires consistent effort over time. By building habits that support these skills, you can create a strong foundation for long-term success in self-leadership.

1. Start Small and Build Momentum

When developing new habits, it's important to start small and gradually build momentum. This approach helps to prevent overwhelm and increases the likelihood of long-term success.

Exercise:

- ❖ Choose one small habit that aligns with your goals and focus on establishing it before moving on to the next.
- ❖ Gradually increase the difficulty or frequency of the habit as it becomes more ingrained in your routine.

Example: If your goal is to meditate daily, start with just five minutes each morning. Once this habit is established, gradually increase the duration until it becomes a regular part of your routine.

2. Use Habit Stacking

Habit stacking is a technique where you attach a new habit to an existing one. By linking the new habit to a well-established routine, you can make it easier to remember and maintain.

Exercise:

- ❖ Identify a habit you already do consistently (e.g., brushing your teeth, making coffee).
- ❖ Attach a new habit to this routine by performing it immediately before or after the existing habit.

Example: If you want to start journaling, do it right after your morning coffee. The existing habit of making coffee acts as a trigger, reminding you to journal.

3. Track Your Progress

Tracking your progress helps you stay motivated and disciplined by providing a visual reminder of your achievements. It also allows you to identify patterns and make adjustments as needed.

Exercise:

- ❖ Choose a method to track your progress, such as a journal, app, or calendar.
- ❖ Record your daily or weekly progress toward your goals and review it regularly.

Example: If you're working on improving your fitness, track your workouts in a journal, noting the exercises you did and how you felt afterward. Reviewing your progress can boost your motivation and help you stay on track.

Translating Self-Discipline and Motivation to Effective Leadership

Self-discipline and motivation are not only essential for personal success but also for effective leadership. Leaders who embody these qualities can inspire and guide others, even in challenging situations.

1. Leading by Example

Leaders who demonstrate self-discipline and motivation set a powerful example for their teams. When team members see their leader consistently pursuing goals, staying focused, and overcoming challenges, they are more likely to adopt these behaviors themselves.

Example: A manager who arrives on time, meets deadlines, and maintains a positive attitude, even during stressful periods, sets a standard for the rest of the team to follow.

Practical Exercises for Building Self-Discipline

Building self-discipline is a gradual process that requires consistent effort. Here are some practical exercises to help you develop and strengthen this critical skill:

1. Goal Setting: The Foundation of Self-Discipline

Setting clear, specific goals is the first step toward developing self-discipline. Goals provide direction and purpose, helping you stay focused on what truly matters.

Exercise:

Identify one short-term and one long-term goal that you want to achieve. Make sure they are specific, measurable, achievable, relevant, and time-bound (SMART goals).

Break down your long-term goal into smaller, actionable steps. Create a timeline for completing each step, and track your progress regularly.

Example: If your long-term goal is to run a marathon, your short-term goals might include running a certain distance each week, improving your diet, and scheduling regular strength training sessions.

2. Habit Formation: Turning Discipline into a Routine

Habits are behaviors that become automatic over time through repetition. By establishing positive habits, you can make self-discipline a natural part of your daily routine.

Exercise:

- Choose one behavior that aligns with your goals (e.g., exercising, reading, or meditating).
- Commit to practicing this behavior at the same time every day for at least 21 days. Consistency is key to forming a habit.

Example: If you want to develop the habit of exercising, schedule a 30-minute workout every morning after waking up. Over time, this routine will become ingrained, making it easier to maintain your discipline.

3. Delayed Gratification: Strengthening Your Willpower

Delayed gratification is the ability to resist immediate rewards in favor of long-term gains. This skill is essential for maintaining self-discipline, especially when faced with temptations.

Exercise:

- Identify an area where you tend to seek immediate gratification (e.g., snacking, procrastinating).
- Practice delaying that gratification by setting a timer for 10 minutes before indulging. Gradually increase the delay as your willpower strengthens.

Example: If you have a habit of snacking between meals, try delaying the urge by drinking water or taking a short walk. Over time, this practice will help you build greater self-control.

4. Positive Reinforcement: Rewarding Disciplined Behavior

Positive reinforcement involves rewarding yourself for making disciplined choices. This helps reinforce the behavior, making it more likely that you'll repeat it in the future.

Exercise:

- ❖ Set up a reward system for completing tasks that require self-discipline. The rewards can be small, such as enjoying a favorite snack or taking a relaxing break.
- ❖ Ensure that the rewards are aligned with your goals and do not undermine your progress.

Example: If you complete a week of planned workouts, reward yourself with a movie night or a special treat. The anticipation of the reward can motivate you to stay disciplined.

Cultivating Motivation: Strategies to Keep You Moving Forward

Motivation is the driving force behind your actions, but it can wane over time. To sustain your motivation, it's important to connect with your deeper reasons for pursuing your goals and to create an environment that supports your aspirations.

1. Connect with Your 'Why': The Deep Root of Motivation

Understanding the underlying reasons behind your goals can provide powerful motivation. Reflect on why these goals are important to you and how achieving they will improve your life.

Exercise:

- ❖ Take some time to journal about your goals and the reasons why they matter to you. Be honest and detailed in your reflections.
- ❖ Keep this journal entry handy and refer to it whenever you feel your motivation waning.

Example: If your goal is to advance in your career, your 'why' might be to provide a better future for your family or to achieve personal fulfillment. Keeping this purpose in mind can motivate you to push through challenges.

2. Visualize Success: Harnessing the Power of Imagination

Visualization is a powerful technique that involves imagining yourself achieving your goals in vivid detail. This mental imagery can create positive emotions and increase your motivation to take action.

Exercise:

- ❖ Spend a few minutes each day visualizing yourself achieving your goals. Imagine how you'll feel, what you'll see, and what you'll hear.
- ❖ Use all your senses to make the visualization as realistic as possible.

Example: If your goal is to write a book, visualize yourself holding the finished product in your hands, feeling proud and accomplished. This positive imagery can help you stay motivated during the writing process.

3. Surround Yourself with Positivity: Creating a Supportive Environment

Your environment and the people you interact with can significantly impact your motivation. Surround yourself with supportive, positive influences that encourage you to stay focused on your goals.

Exercise:

Identify any negative influences in your environment (e.g., unsupportive friends, cluttered workspace) and take steps to minimize their impact.

Seek out positive influences, such as joining a community of like-minded individuals or following inspiring role models.

Example: If you're trying to eat healthier, surround yourself with friends who share your goals, or join an online group where members share tips and recipes. The support and encouragement you receive can boost your motivation.

4. Break down Goals and Celebrate Milestones: Keeping the Momentum Going

Large goals can sometimes feel overwhelming, leading to a loss of motivation. By breaking them down into smaller, more manageable milestones, you can maintain a sense of progress and achievement.

Exercise:

- Divide your larger goals into smaller milestones with specific deadlines.
- Celebrate each milestone you achieve, no matter how small.

Example: If your goal is to start a business, break it down into milestones like developing a business plan, securing funding, and launching the website. Celebrate each milestone with a small reward, like treating yourself to your favorite snack or taking a day off.

Translating Self-Discipline and Motivation into Effective Leadership

Self-discipline and motivation are not only essential for personal success but also for effective leadership. Leaders who embody these qualities can inspire and guide others, even in challenging situations.

1. Leading by Example: The Power of Role Modeling

Leaders who demonstrate self-discipline and motivation set a powerful example for their teams. When team members see their leader consistently pursuing goals, staying focused, and overcoming challenges, they are more likely to adopt these behaviors themselves.

Example: A manager who arrives on time, meets deadlines, and maintains a positive attitude, even during stressful periods, sets a standard for the rest of the team to follow.

2. Empowering Others: Inspiring Self-Discipline in Your Team

Leaders can use their own self-discipline and motivation to inspire and empower their team members. By encouraging others to set goals, develop routines, and practice delayed gratification, leaders can foster a culture of discipline and motivation within their organization.

Exercise:

- ❖ Encourage team members to set their own goals and create personal development plans. Provide support and resources to help them succeed.
- ❖ Recognize and celebrate team members' achievements, reinforcing the value of discipline and motivation.

Example: A leader who consistently recognizes and rewards team members for their disciplined efforts and achievements fosters a culture where everyone is motivated to perform at their best.

3. Creating a Motivating Environment: Fostering a Culture of Achievement

Leaders play a crucial role in creating an environment that motivates and energizes their teams. This involves setting clear expectations, providing regular feedback, and fostering a sense of purpose and belonging.

Exercise:

- ❖ Set clear, achievable goals for your team and communicate them effectively. Ensure that each team member understands their role in achieving these goals.

❖ Provide regular feedback and recognition, celebrating both individual and team successes.

Example: A leader who regularly communicates the team's progress toward its goals and acknowledges the contributions of each member creates a motivating environment where everyone feels valued and driven to succeed.

The Path to Self-Leadership

Developing self-discipline and motivation is a journey that requires consistent effort and commitment. By setting clear goals, establishing positive habits, and maintaining a strong connection to your purpose, you can cultivate these foundational skills and apply them to all areas of your life.

As you build self-discipline and motivation, you'll not only enhance your ability to lead yourself but also inspire and guide others. Whether you're leading a team, pursuing personal goals, or striving to make a positive impact in your community, these skills will empower you to achieve your full potential and create lasting.

Developing Self-Discipline and Motivation: A Comprehensive Guide to Self-Leadership

As a personal development coach, one of the most crucial aspects of self-leadership I emphasize is the cultivation of self-discipline and motivation. These foundational skills empower individuals to take control of their lives, achieve their goals, and lead others effectively. This guide will provide you with practical exercises, habit-building strategies, and real-world examples to help you develop these essential qualities.

Understanding Self-Discipline and Motivation

Self-discipline is the ability to control your impulses, emotions, and behaviors to achieve long-term goals. It's about making choices that align with your values and objectives, even when they're not the easiest or most immediately gratifying options. Self-discipline enables you to stay focused on your path and resist distractions or temptations that could derail your progress.

Motivation, on the other hand, is the driving force behind your actions. It's what gets you started on a task and keeps you going, even when challenges arise. Motivation can come from internal sources, like personal values and goals (intrinsic motivation), or external sources, like rewards and recognition (extrinsic motivation).

Together, self-discipline and motivation form a powerful duo that fuels self-leadership. While motivation gets you started, self-discipline keeps you on track, ensuring that you follow through on your commitments and achieve your goals.

Building Self-Discipline: Practical Exercises

Developing self-discipline is a gradual process that requires consistent practice. Here are some practical exercises to help you build this crucial skill:

Set Clear Goals

Clear, specific goals provide direction and purpose. Without clear goals, it's easy to become distracted or lose focus. Start by defining what you want to achieve, both in the short term and long term. Break down larger goals into smaller, manageable tasks that you can work on consistently.

Exercise:

Write down your top three goals for the next six months. For each goal, list the specific actions you need to take to achieve them.

Break these actions down into daily or weekly tasks and prioritize them based on their importance.

Example: If your goal is to improve your physical fitness, your smaller tasks might include scheduling three weekly workouts, preparing healthy meals in advance, and tracking your progress.

Create a Routine

Routines help to automate discipline by turning desired behaviors into habits. When you consistently perform certain actions at the same time each day, they become ingrained in your routine, requiring less mental effort to maintain.

Exercise:

- Identify key areas where you want to improve your discipline (e.g., exercise, work productivity, healthy eating).
- Design a daily routine that incorporates these activities at specific times.
- Commit to following this routine for at least 21 days to help establish new habits.

Example: If you want to become more disciplined in your work, you might set aside the first two hours of each workday for focused, uninterrupted tasks, with a 10-minute break afterward as a reward.

Practice Delayed Gratification

Delayed gratification is the ability to resist the temptation of an immediate reward in favor of a larger, long-term benefit. It's a key component of self-discipline and can be developed through practice.

Exercise:

- Identify a habit where you typically seek immediate gratification (e.g., snacking, procrastinating).
- Challenge yourself to delay that gratification by 10 minutes, then gradually increase the delay over time.
- Use this time to focus on the long-term benefits of resisting the temptation.

Example: If you're trying to cut down on unhealthy snacks, delay eating a treat by 10 minutes while you drink a glass of water or distract yourself with another task. Over time, this practice will strengthen your ability to delay gratification in other areas.

Use Positive Reinforcement

Positive reinforcement involves rewarding yourself for making disciplined choices. This reinforces the behavior and makes it more likely that you'll repeat it in the future.

Exercise:

- ❖ Set up a reward system for completing your daily or weekly tasks. The rewards can be small, like taking a break or enjoying a favorite activity.
- ❖ Make sure the rewards are aligned with your goals and do not undermine your progress.

Example: If you complete all your planned workouts for the week, reward yourself with a relaxing activity, like watching a movie or taking a long bath. The anticipation of the reward can motivate you to stay disciplined.

Cultivating Motivation: Strategies and Tips

While self-discipline keeps you on track, motivation provides the energy and enthusiasm to pursue your goals. Here's how to cultivate and sustain motivation:

Connect with Your 'Why'

Understanding the deeper reasons behind your goals can provide powerful motivation. Reflect on why your goals are important to you and how achieving they will improve your life.

Exercise:

- ❖ Take some time to journal about your goals and why they matter to you. Be honest and detailed in your reflections.
- ❖ Keep this journal entry handy and refer to it whenever you feel your motivation waning.

Example: If your goal is to advance in your career, your 'why' might be to provide a better future for your family or to achieve personal fulfillment. Keeping this purpose in mind can motivate you to push through challenges.

Visualize Success

Visualization is a technique where you imagine yourself achieving your goals in vivid detail. This mental imagery can create positive emotions and increase your motivation to take action.

Exercise:

- ❖ Spend a few minutes each day visualizing yourself achieving your goals. Imagine how you'll feel, what you'll see, and what you'll hear.
- ❖ Use all your senses to make the visualization as realistic as possible.

Example: If your goal is to run a marathon, visualize yourself crossing the finish line, feeling strong and accomplished. This positive imagery can help you stay motivated during training.

Surround Yourself with Positivity

Your environment and the people you interact with can significantly impact your motivation. Surround yourself with supportive, positive influences that encourage you to stay focused on your goals.

Exercise:

Identify any negative influences in your environment (e.g., unsupportive friends, cluttered workspace) and take steps to minimize their impact.

Seek out positive influences, such as joining a community of like-minded individuals or following inspiring role models.

Example: If you're trying to eat healthier, surround yourself with friends who share your goals, or join an online group where members share tips and recipes. The support and encouragement you receive can boost your motivation.

Break Down Goals and Celebrate Milestones

Large goals can sometimes feel overwhelming, leading to a loss of motivation. By breaking them down into smaller, more manageable milestones, you can maintain a sense of progress and achievement.

Exercise:

- ❖ Divide your larger goals into smaller milestones with specific deadlines.
- ❖ Celebrate each milestone you achieve, no matter how small.

Example: If your goal is to write a book, break it down into milestones like completing the outline, writing each chapter, and editing. Celebrate each milestone with a small reward, like treating yourself to your favorite snack or taking a day off.

Habit-Building Strategies for Long-Term Success

Developing self-discipline and motivation requires consistent effort over time. By building habits that support these skills, you can create a strong foundation for long-term success in self-leadership.

Start Small and Build Momentum

When developing new habits, it's important to start small and gradually build momentum. This approach helps to prevent overwhelm and increases the likelihood of long-term success.

Exercise:

- ❖ Choose one small habit that aligns with your goals and focus on establishing it before moving on to the next.
- ❖ Gradually increase the difficulty or frequency of the habit as it becomes more ingrained in your routine.

Example: If your goal is to meditate daily, start with just five minutes each morning. Once this habit is established, gradually increase the duration until it becomes a regular part of your routine.

Use Habit Stacking

Habit stacking is a technique where you attach a new habit to an existing one. By linking the new habit to a well-established routine, you can make it easier to remember and maintain.

Exercise:

Identify a habit you already do consistently (e.g., brushing your teeth, making coffee).

Attach a new habit to this routine by performing it immediately before or after the existing habit.

Example: If you want to start journaling, do it right after your morning coffee. The existing habit of making coffee acts as a trigger, reminding you to journal.

Track Your Progress

Tracking your progress helps you stay motivated and disciplined by providing a visual reminder of your achievements. It also allows you to identify patterns and make adjustments as needed.

Exercise:

- ❖ Choose a method to track your progress, such as a journal, app, or calendar.
- ❖ Record your daily or weekly progress toward your goals and review it regularly.

Example: If you're working on improving your fitness, track your workouts in a journal, noting the exercises you did and how you felt afterward. Reviewing your progress can boost your motivation and help you stay on track.

Translating Self-Discipline and Motivation to Effective Leadership

Self-discipline and motivation are not only essential for personal success but also for effective leadership. Leaders who embody these qualities can inspire and guide others, even in challenging situations.

Leading by Example

Leaders who demonstrate self-discipline and motivation set a powerful example for their teams. When team members see their leader consistently pursuing goals, staying focused, and overcoming challenges, they are more likely to adopt these behaviors themselves.

Example: A manager who arrives on time, meets deadlines, and maintains a positive attitude, even during stressful periods, sets a standard for the rest of the team to follow.

Empowering Others

Leaders can use their own self-discipline and motivation to inspire and empower their team members. By encouraging others to set goals, develop routines, and practice delayed gratification, leaders can foster a culture of discipline.

Developing Self-Discipline and Motivation: A Comprehensive Guide to Self-Leadership

Self-discipline and motivation are foundational skills that form the bedrock of self-leadership. As a personal development coach, I emphasize these qualities because they empower individuals to take control of their lives, achieve their goals, and effectively lead others. This guide offers detailed insights, practical exercises, and real-world examples to help you develop and harness these essential traits.

Understanding Self-Discipline and Motivation

Self-discipline is the ability to control your impulses, emotions, and behaviors to stay aligned with long-term goals. It's about making choices that support your objectives, even when easier or more tempting alternatives are available. Self-discipline keeps you focused and resilient in the face of challenges and distractions.

Motivation is the internal or external drive that compels you to take action. Intrinsic motivation comes from personal satisfaction, while extrinsic motivation is driven by rewards or recognition. Effective self-leadership requires both—motivation to get started and self-discipline to see things through.

Building Self-Discipline: Practical Exercises

Developing self-discipline is a process that involves consistent practice and intentional effort.

Below are some exercises designed to help you cultivate this vital skill?

Setting Clear Goals

Clear goals are essential for direction and purpose. Without them, it's easy to become distracted or lose focus. Start by defining what you want to achieve in both the short term and long term. Break down larger goals into smaller, manageable tasks.

Exercise:

- ❖ Write down your top three goals for the next six months.
- ❖ List the specific actions required to achieve each goal.
- ❖ Break these actions into daily or weekly tasks and prioritize them.

Example: If your goal is to improve physical fitness, your tasks might include scheduling workouts, preparing healthy meals, and tracking your progress.

Creating a Routine

Routines help transform disciplined behaviors into habits. Consistently performing specific actions at the same time each day can automate discipline, requiring less mental effort.

Exercise:

- ❖ Identify areas where you want to improve your discipline (e.g., exercise, productivity).
- ❖ Design a daily routine that includes these activities.
- ❖ Commit to following this routine for at least 21 days to establish new habits.

Example: If you aim to enhance work productivity, set aside the first two hours of your day for focused, uninterrupted tasks, with a 10-minute break afterward as a reward.

Practicing Delayed Gratification

Delayed gratification is the ability to resist immediate rewards in favor of long-term benefits. It's a key component of self-discipline that can be strengthened through practice.

Exercise:

- ❖ Identify a habit where you typically seek immediate gratification (e.g., snacking, procrastinating).

- ❖ Challenge yourself to delay gratification by 10 minutes, gradually increasing the delay over time.
- ❖ Focus on the long-term benefits of resisting the temptation.

Example: If you tend to snack between meals, delay eating a treat by drinking water or engaging in another task. Over time, this will help build your capacity for delayed gratification.

Using Positive Reinforcement

Positive reinforcement involves rewarding yourself for disciplined behavior, reinforcing the likelihood of repeating it.

Exercise:

Set up a reward system for completing tasks that require discipline. Rewards can be small, like enjoying a favorite activity.

Ensure that rewards align with your goals and don't undermine your progress.

Example: After completing a week of planned workouts, reward yourself with a relaxing activity like a movie night or a special treat.

Cultivating Motivation: Strategies and Tips

While self-discipline keeps you on track, motivation fuels your journey. Here's how to sustain and enhance your motivation:

Connecting with Your 'Why'

Understanding the deeper reasons behind your goals provides powerful motivation. Reflect on why these goals matter and how achieving them will improve your life.

Exercise:

- ❖ Journal about your goals and the reasons they're important to you.
- ❖ Refer to this journal entry whenever your motivation wanes.

Example: If your goal is career advancement, your 'why' might be to provide a better future for your family or achieve personal fulfillment. Keeping this purpose in mind can motivate you to push through challenges.

Visualizing Success

Visualization involves imagining yourself achieving your goals in vivid detail. This mental imagery can create positive emotions and boost motivation.

Exercise:

- ❖ Spend a few minutes each day visualizing your success. Imagine how it feels, what you see, and what you hear.
- ❖ Make the visualization as realistic as possible.

Example: If your goal is to write a book, visualize holding the finished product, feeling proud and accomplished. This positive imagery can help sustain motivation throughout the writing process.

Surrounding Yourself with Positivity

Your environment and the people around you significantly impact your motivation. Surround yourself with supportive, positive influences that encourage your progress.

Exercise:

- ❖ Identify and minimize negative influences in your environment (e.g., unsupportive friends, clutter).
- ❖ Seek out positive influences, like joining a community of like-minded individuals or following inspiring role models.

Example: If you aim to eat healthier, surround yourself with friends who share your goals or join an online group where members exchange tips and recipes. The support you receive can strengthen your motivation.

Breaking Down Goals and Celebrating Milestones

Large goals can feel overwhelming, leading to a loss of motivation. Breaking them into smaller milestones provides a sense of progress and achievement.

Exercise:

- ❖ Divide larger goals into smaller milestones with specific deadlines.
- ❖ Celebrate each milestone, no matter how small.

Example: If your goal is to start a business, break it into milestones like developing a business plan, securing funding, and launching the website. Celebrate each milestone with a small reward, like a day off or a special treat.

Habit-Building Strategies for Long-Term Success

Long-term success in self-discipline and motivation comes from consistent effort. By building habits that support these skills, you create a strong foundation for ongoing self-leadership.

Starting Small and Building Momentum

When developing new habits, start small to prevent overwhelm and increase the likelihood of success.

Exercise:

- ❖ Choose one small habit aligned with your goals and focus on establishing it before moving on to the next.
- ❖ Gradually increase the difficulty or frequency as the habit becomes ingrained.

Example: If your goal is to meditate daily, start with five minutes each morning. Gradually increase the duration until it's a regular part of your routine.

Using Habit Stacking

Habit stacking involves attaching a new habit to an existing one, making it easier to remember and maintain.

Exercise:

- Identify a consistent habit (e.g., brushing your teeth, making coffee).
- Attach a new habit to this routine by performing it immediately before or after the existing habit.

Example: If you want to start journaling, do it right after your morning coffee. The existing habit of making coffee serves as a reminder to journal.

Tracking Your Progress

Tracking progress helps maintain motivation and discipline by visually reminding you of your achievements. It also allows you to identify patterns and make necessary adjustments.

Exercise:

- ❖ Choose a method to track your progress, such as a journal, app, or calendar.
- ❖ Record daily or weekly progress and review it regularly.

Example: If your goal is fitness, track workouts in a journal, noting exercises and how you felt afterward. Reviewing progress can boost motivation and help you stay on track.

Translating Self-Discipline and Motivation into Leadership

Self-discipline and motivation are not only essential for personal success but also for effective leadership. Leaders who embody these qualities can inspire and guide others, even in challenging situations.

Leading by Example

Leaders who demonstrate self-discipline and motivation set a powerful example for their teams. When team members see their leader consistently pursuing goals, staying focused, and overcoming challenges, they are more likely to adopt these behaviors themselves.

Example: A manager who arrives on time, meets deadlines, and maintains a positive attitude, even during stressful periods, sets a standard for the rest of the team to follow.

Empowering Others

Leaders can use their own self-discipline and motivation to inspire and empower their team members. By encouraging others to set goals, develop routines, and practice delayed gratification, leaders foster a culture of discipline and motivation within their organization.

Exercise:

- ❖ Encourage team members to set their own goals and create personal development plans. Provide support and resources to help them succeed.
- ❖ Recognize and celebrate team members' achievements, reinforcing the value of discipline and motivation.

Example: A leader who consistently recognizes and rewards team members for their disciplined efforts and achievements fosters a culture where everyone is motivated to perform at their best.

Creating a Motivating Environment

Leaders play a crucial role in creating an environment that motivates and energizes their teams. This involves setting clear expectations, providing regular feedback, and fostering a sense of purpose and belonging.

Exercise:

- ❖ Set clear, achievable goals for your team and communicate them effectively. Ensure that each team member understands their role in achieving these goals.
- ❖ Provide regular feedback and recognition, celebrating both individual and team successes.

Example: A leader who regularly communicates the team's progress toward its goals and acknowledges the contributions of each member creates a motivating environment where everyone feels valued and driven to succeed.

CREATING A PERSONAL LEADERSHIP PLAN

Developing a personal leadership plan is a strategic approach to enhancing your leadership skills, achieving your goals, and growing both personally and professionally. This detailed guide will walk you through the process, from setting clear objectives to tracking progress and adapting your plan over time. By following these steps, you'll build a robust framework for continuous improvement as a leader.

Step 1: Self-Assessment

Before setting goals, it's crucial to understand where you currently stand as a leader. Self-assessment involves reflecting on your strengths, weaknesses, values, and leadership style.

Actionable Steps:

Reflect on Past Experiences: Think about situations where you've led successfully and where you've struggled. Identify patterns in your behavior and decision-making.

Seek Feedback: Ask colleagues, mentors, or team members for honest feedback on your leadership style. Consider using formal tools like 360-degree feedback surveys.

Assess Your Values and Beliefs: Consider what drives you as a leader. Understanding your core values will help align your leadership style with your true self.

Example: A manager might discover through feedback that they excel at strategic planning but need to improve their interpersonal communication. This insight forms the foundation for setting meaningful leadership goals.

Step 2: Goal Setting

With a clear understanding of your current leadership profile, the next step is to set specific, measurable, achievable, relevant, and time-bound (SMART) goals. These goals should align with both your personal aspirations and your organization's needs.

Actionable Steps:

Identify Long-Term Goals: Determine where you want to be in your leadership journey in the next 5 to 10 years.

Set Short-Term Milestones: Break down long-term goals into shorter, actionable steps that can be achieved within a year or less.

Align with Organizational Goals: Ensure your leadership goals support the broader objectives of your team or organization.

Example: A goal could be to "Improve team collaboration by implementing regular feedback sessions within the next six months." This goal is specific, measurable, and directly supports both personal development and team success.

Step 3: Develop a Learning Plan

To achieve your leadership goals, you'll need to acquire new skills and knowledge. A learning plan outlines the resources, courses, and experiences you'll engage in to develop these competencies.

Actionable Steps:

Identify Skill Gaps: Based on your goals, determine which skills you need to develop. This could include soft skills like communication or hard skills like financial management.

Choose Learning Resources: Select relevant books, online courses, workshops, or mentoring opportunities that will help you acquire these skills.

Create a Learning Schedule: Plan when and how you'll engage with these learning resources, ensuring that it fits into your daily routine.

Example: If a leader aims to improve their emotional intelligence, they might enroll in a course on emotional intelligence, read related books, and practice mindfulness techniques daily.

Step 4: Implementation and Action

With your goals set and learning plan in place, it's time to take action. Implementation is about putting your plan into practice and consistently working towards your objectives.

Actionable Steps:

Prioritize Actions: Determine which goals or skills to focus on first, and start implementing your learning plan.

Apply Learning in Real Time: As you acquire new skills, look for opportunities to apply them in your daily leadership role. This could be through taking on new projects, leading meetings, or mentoring others.

Stay Consistent: Establish a routine that allows you to consistently work on your leadership goals, balancing your current responsibilities with your development plan.

Example: A leader working on communication skills might begin by leading team meetings, applying active listening, and seeking feedback on their communication style.

Step 5: Tracking Progress

Regularly tracking your progress ensures that you stay on course and make necessary adjustments to your plan. It also helps you celebrate small victories and stay motivated.

Actionable Steps:

Set Benchmarks: Define key indicators of success for each goal, such as improved team performance or increased self-confidence.

Review Progress Regularly: Schedule monthly or quarterly reviews of your goals and learning plan. Reflect on what's working and what needs adjustment.

Document Achievements: Keep a journal or digital log of your accomplishments and setbacks. This will provide valuable insights over time.

Example: If a leader's goal is to enhance team collaboration, they might track progress by measuring the frequency and quality of team interactions and gathering feedback from team members.

Step 6: Adapting the Plan

Leadership development is a dynamic process that requires flexibility. As you progress, you'll need to adapt your plan to reflect changes in your role, organization, or personal life.

Actionable Steps:

Evaluate and Reflect: At the end of each quarter, assess whether your goals are still relevant and whether your strategies are effective.

Adjust Goals: Modify your goals based on your progress and any new challenges or opportunities that arise.

Seek New Learning Opportunities: As you develop new skills, identify additional areas for growth and update your learning plan accordingly.

Example: If a leader achieves a significant milestone, like improving team communication, they might set a new goal to enhance their strategic thinking abilities, adapting their learning plan to include new resources and experiences.

Step 7: Review and Reflect

At the end of your leadership development cycle, conduct a comprehensive review of your progress. This reflection will help you recognize your growth, identify areas for further improvement, and set the stage for the next phase of your development.

Actionable Steps:

Analyze Results: Look back at your original goals and assess how well you've met them. Consider both quantitative and qualitative outcomes.

Gather Feedback: Seek input from colleagues, mentors, or coaches on how your leadership has evolved.

Celebrate Achievements: Acknowledge the progress you've made and the challenges you've overcome.

Plan for the Future: Use your reflections to set new goals and begin the next cycle of your leadership development.

Example: A leader who has successfully built a more collaborative team environment might now focus on enhancing innovation within the team, setting new goals, and identifying new learning opportunities.

EMOTIONAL INTELLIGENCE AND LEADERSHIP

In leadership, especially when one lacks formal authority, emotional intelligence (EI) becomes a powerful tool. Emotional intelligence is the ability to recognize, understand, and manage our own emotions while also being sensitive to the emotions of others. It plays a crucial role in how leaders influence, communicate, and interact with their teams. When traditional authority is absent, leveraging EI can bridge the gap, enabling leaders to inspire, motivate, and guide others effectively. This comprehensive guide explores how key components of EI—self-awareness, empathy, and social skills—can be harnessed for leadership, providing detailed examples of how these qualities have been successfully applied.

HARNESSING EI FOR EFFECTIVE LEADERSHIP

Emotional intelligence is comprised of several components, each contributing to a leader's ability to manage relationships, navigate social complexities, and make decisions that respect both personal and organizational needs. The core components of EI include:

Self-Awareness: Understanding one's own emotions, strengths, weaknesses, and the impact of these factors on others.

Self-Regulation: The ability to control or redirect disruptive emotions and impulses.

Motivation: A passion to work for reasons beyond money or status; a propensity to pursue goals with energy and persistence.

Empathy: The ability to understand the emotional makeup of other people; skill in treating people according to their emotional reactions.

Social Skills: Proficiency in managing relationships and building networks; an ability to find common ground and build rapport.

The Role of Self-Awareness in Leadership without Authority

Self-awareness is the foundation of emotional intelligence. It involves being in tune with your emotions and understanding how they affect your thoughts and actions. Leaders who are self-aware are better equipped to recognize how their emotions influence their interactions with others. This self-knowledge allows them to communicate more effectively and to be more adaptable in various situations.

Practical Application: A self-aware leader in a project team, without the formal title of manager, may notice that stress is causing them to become impatient with team members. Recognizing this, the leader can take steps to manage their stress, ensuring that their impatience doesn't negatively impact the team's morale or performance. By addressing their own emotional responses, they model calmness and control, which can influence the entire team's atmosphere.

Example: Consider Satya Nadella, CEO of Microsoft, who is known for his high emotional intelligence. Nadella's self-awareness is evident in his leadership style, where he emphasizes empathy, humility, and a growth mindset. These qualities have helped him steer Microsoft through significant cultural and strategic changes, earning him respect and influence far beyond his formal authority.

Empathy: The Cornerstone of Influence

Empathy is the ability to understand and share the feelings of others. It's essential for leaders who seek to influence without authority because it builds trust, fosters strong relationships, and encourages open communication. Empathetic leaders are able to connect with their team members on a personal level, understanding their needs, concerns, and motivations.

Practical Application: In a scenario where a leader is not formally in charge, empathy allows them to tune into the emotions and concerns of their colleagues. For instance, if a team member is struggling with a heavy workload, an empathetic leader might offer support, suggest delegation strategies, or simply listen to the person's concerns. This support can build strong bonds of trust and loyalty, which are crucial when the leader lacks formal power.

Example: Indra Nooyi, former CEO of PepsiCo, is often cited as an example of a leader with strong empathetic abilities. Nooyi made it a point to understand her employees' lives outside of work, regularly writing personal notes to their families. Her empathetic leadership style helped create a loyal and motivated workforce, contributing to PepsiCo's long-term success.

Social Skills: Building Networks and Managing Relationships

Social skills are the tools that leaders use to manage relationships, build networks, and navigate social complexities. Leaders with strong social skills can influence others, not through authority, but through their ability to communicate effectively, resolve conflicts, and inspire collaboration.

Practical Application: A leader without formal authority might use their social skills to build a coalition of supporters within their organization. By fostering relationships across different departments and levels, they can gather support for their ideas and initiatives. They might organize informal meetings, led by example in collaborative projects, or simply be the person who listens and mediates in conflicts. Over time, these efforts can create a network of influence that extends beyond their official role.

Example: Bill Gates, during his time leading Microsoft, effectively used his social skills to influence and drive the company's success. Gates built strong relationships with key players in the industry, often collaborating and negotiating to achieve Microsoft's goals. Even when Gates was not the formal authority in certain ventures, his social acumen allowed him to guide the direction of the industry as a whole.

Self-Regulation: Managing Emotions for Consistent Leadership

Self-regulation refers to the ability to control or redirect one's emotions and impulses. It's particularly important for leaders who lack formal authority because it helps them maintain composure, even in challenging situations. Leaders who can regulate their emotions are able to respond to setbacks and conflicts with a level head, maintaining the respect and trust of their peers.

Practical Application: Imagine a leader in a cross-functional team where they are not the official supervisor. A critical project faces an unexpected setback, and tensions rise. Instead of reacting with frustration, a self-regulated leader remains calm, assesses the situation objectively, and works with the team to find a solution. By staying composed, they set a tone of resilience and problem-solving, which can positively influence the entire team's response.

Example: Angela Merkel, former Chancellor of Germany, is known for her calm and measured responses, even in the face of crises. Merkel's ability to self-regulate allowed her to lead Germany through numerous challenges, from economic crises to political upheavals, earning her a reputation as a steady and reliable leader.

Motivation: Driving Passion and Persistence

Motivation in the context of emotional intelligence is the inner drive to achieve goals, often beyond the expectation of rewards or recognition. For leaders without formal authority, intrinsic motivation can be the force that propels them to overcome obstacles and persist in their efforts to influence and lead.

Practical Application: A motivated leader might take the initiative to lead a project that aligns with their values and passions, even if it's not directly within their job description. They could volunteer to spearhead a new initiative or mentor others, driven by the desire to make a meaningful impact. Their enthusiasm and commitment can inspire others to join them, creating momentum that doesn't rely on formal authority.

Example: Nelson Mandela is a profound example of a leader whose motivation led him to inspire change without formal authority for much of his life. Despite being imprisoned, Mandela's unwavering commitment to his cause motivated others to join the anti-apartheid movement, eventually leading to significant social and political changes in South Africa.

Case Study: Emotional Intelligence in Action

Let's consider a case study of a mid-level manager named Sarah, who used emotional intelligence to lead her team effectively, despite lacking formal authority over them.

Background: Sarah was a project manager at a tech company, leading a team composed of members from different departments. She was not their direct supervisor, but she was responsible for coordinating their efforts to ensure the project's success.

Challenges: The team faced significant challenges, including tight deadlines, conflicting priorities, and interpersonal conflicts. Sarah realized that she needed to lead without authority, relying on her emotional intelligence to guide the team.

Application of EI:

Self-Awareness: Sarah first reflected on her own strengths and weaknesses. She recognized that her calm demeanor was a strength, but she needed to be more assertive in communicating expectations.

Empathy: Sarah took the time to understand each team member's perspective. She regularly checked in with them, showing genuine concern for their well-being and understanding their individual challenges.

Social Skills: Sarah used her social skills to mediate conflicts within the team. She organized regular team-building activities and open forums where members could express their concerns. Her ability to listen and facilitate discussions helped resolve tensions.

Self-Regulation: During high-pressure moments, Sarah maintained her composure, helping to keep the team focused and motivated. She was transparent about challenges but always emphasized finding solutions rather than assigning blame.

Motivation: Sarah's passion for the project was evident in her work ethic. She often went the extra mile, and her dedication inspired the team to do the same.

Outcome: Sarah's use of emotional intelligence created a cohesive and motivated team, leading to the successful completion of the project. Her leadership was recognized by her peers and superiors, resulting in a formal promotion shortly after the project's conclusion.

MANAGING STRESS AND BUILDING RESILIENCE

Leadership, while rewarding, comes with a unique set of challenges that can lead to significant stress. The pressure to meet deadlines, manage teams, and achieve organizational goals often creates an environment ripe for stress. However, effective leaders must develop resilience to maintain their performance and well-being under pressure. This guide provides a detailed approach to managing stress and building resilience through techniques like mindfulness, time management, and cognitive reframing, ensuring leaders can thrive even in demanding situations.

Understanding Stress and Its Impact on Leadership

Stress is a natural response to challenging situations, but chronic stress can have detrimental effects on a leader's ability to make decisions, communicate effectively, and maintain relationships with their team. When leaders are overwhelmed by stress, it can lead to burnout, decreased productivity, and even affect the morale of their team. Therefore, managing stress is not just about personal well-being; it's also about maintaining leadership effectiveness and the health of the entire organization.

Mindfulness: Cultivating Present-Moment Awareness

Mindfulness is the practice of staying present and fully engaging with the current moment. It helps leaders reduce stress by allowing them to focus on the task at hand rather than worrying about future challenges or ruminating on past mistakes.

Practical Application:

Mindful Breathing: Start by dedicating a few minutes each day to mindful breathing exercises. Focus on your breath, noticing the sensation of air entering and leaving your body. This practice helps to calm the mind and reduce immediate stress.

Body Scan Meditation: Another effective mindfulness technique is the body scan, where you mentally scan your body from head to toe, noticing any areas of tension and consciously relaxing them. This practice not only reduces stress but also increases awareness of how stress affects your body.

Example: A leader facing a high-stakes meeting might take five minutes before the meeting to practice mindful breathing. This short exercise can help them enter the meeting with a calm and focused mindset, better equipped to handle any challenges that arise.

Time Management: Prioritizing Tasks to Reduce Overwhelm

Time management is crucial for reducing stress and increasing productivity. Effective time management allows leaders to prioritize tasks, allocate time efficiently, and avoid the stress of last-minute work.

Practical Application:

The Eisenhower Matrix: This tool helps leaders categorize tasks based on urgency and importance, allowing them to focus on what truly matters. Tasks are divided into four categories: urgent and important, important but not urgent, urgent but not important, and neither urgent nor important. By focusing on the first two categories, leaders can manage their time more effectively and reduce stress.

Time Blocking: Allocate specific blocks of time for different tasks throughout the day. This technique helps ensure that important tasks receive the attention they deserve and prevents the stress of juggling multiple tasks simultaneously.

Example: A leader overwhelmed with a long to-do list can use the Eisenhower Matrix to identify the most critical tasks. By focusing on completing these tasks first, they can reduce their stress levels and feel a sense of accomplishment.

Cognitive Reframing: Changing the Way You Perceive Challenges

Cognitive reframing is a psychological technique that involves changing the way you interpret and respond to stressful situations. By reframing negative thoughts into more positive or neutral ones, leaders can reduce the impact of stress on their mental health.

Practical Application:

Challenge vs. Threat Mindset: Encourage yourself to view stressful situations as challenges rather than threats. For example, instead of thinking, "This project is going to be a disaster if it doesn't go well," reframe it as, "This project is an opportunity to showcase my team's strengths."

Positive Self-Talk: Replace negative self-talk with positive affirmations. For example, instead of thinking, "I can't handle this pressure," remind yourself, "I have the skills and resources to manage this situation effectively."

Example: A leader facing a critical presentation might initially feel anxious and doubt their ability to perform. By using cognitive reframing, they can shift their mindset to view the presentation as an opportunity to demonstrate their expertise and contribute to the organization's success.

Building Resilience: The Foundation of Sustainable Leadership

Resilience is the ability to bounce back from adversity and maintain performance under pressure. For leaders, resilience is essential not only for their own well-being but also for setting a positive example for their team.

Practical Application:

Develop a Growth Mindset: Embrace challenges as opportunities for growth rather than setbacks. Leaders with a growth mindset view failures as learning experiences and are more likely to persevere in the face of difficulties.

Cultivate Strong Relationships: Building a support network of colleagues, mentors, and friends provides leaders with emotional support and guidance during tough times. These relationships can act as a buffer against stress and help leaders maintain resilience.

Practice Self-Care: Resilience is closely linked to overall well-being. Leaders should prioritize self-care activities such as regular exercise, adequate sleep, and healthy eating to maintain their physical and mental health.

Example: A leader who practices resilience might face a major project setback but instead of being demoralized, they view it as a chance to learn and improve. They reach out to their network for advice, implement new strategies, and emerge stronger and more confident.

Integrating Stress Management and Resilience Practices

For leaders to effectively manage stress and build resilience, it's essential to integrate these practices into their daily routines. Here's how these techniques can work together to create a comprehensive approach to leadership well-being:

Morning Mindfulness Routine: Start the day with a mindfulness exercise, such as mindful breathing or a short meditation session. This sets a calm and focused tone for the day, helping leaders approach their tasks with clarity.

Daily Time Management Check-In: Use the Eisenhower Matrix to plan the day's tasks, ensuring that high-priority items are addressed first. Incorporate time blocking to allocate dedicated periods for important work, meetings, and breaks.

Midday Reframing Practice: During a lunch break or a quiet moment, take a few minutes to practice cognitive reframing. Reflect on any stressors that have arisen and consciously reframe them in a more positive light.

End-of-Day Reflection: End the day with a reflection on successes and areas for improvement. Acknowledge challenges faced, celebrate small victories, and reinforce the growth mindset. This reflection helps leaders process the day's events and prepare for the next day with a positive outlook.

Example: A leader implementing these practices might begin their day with a ten-minute mindfulness meditation, followed by a time management session where they outline their top priorities. Throughout the day, they consciously reframe challenges, and at the end of the day, they reflect on what they've learned and how they can apply it moving forward. This routine not only reduces stress but also builds the resilience needed to lead effectively.

Real-World Examples of Resilient Leaders

To illustrate the effectiveness of these techniques, let's look at some real-world examples of leaders who have successfully managed stress and built resilience:

Sheryl Sandberg, COO of Facebook: Sandberg is known for her resilience, particularly in the face of personal and professional challenges. After the sudden death of her husband, Sandberg openly discussed her journey through grief and how she used mindfulness, a strong support network, and a growth mindset to cope. Her ability to lead Facebook through periods of significant change while managing her personal loss is a testament to her resilience.

Winston Churchill, Former Prime Minister of the United Kingdom: During World War II, Churchill faced immense pressure as he led the UK through one of its darkest periods. Despite the overwhelming stress, Churchill maintained his resilience through practices such as maintaining a strict daily routine, engaging in hobbies like painting, and staying connected with his support network. His leadership helped boost the morale of the British people and ultimately contributed to the Allied victory.

Oprah Winfrey, Media Mogul: Oprah Winfrey's journey to becoming one of the most successful media personalities in the world was fraught with challenges. Winfrey has often spoken about the importance of mindfulness, positive thinking, and resilience in her life. She practices daily meditation and gratitude, which help her manage stress and stay focused on her goals. Winfrey's resilience has been key to her ability to overcome adversity and achieve lasting success.

Conclusion: The Path to Resilient Leadership

Managing stress and building resilience are essential skills for leaders who want to maintain their effectiveness under pressure. By incorporating practices such as mindfulness, time management, and cognitive reframing into their daily routines, leaders can not only reduce stress but also strengthen their ability to bounce back from challenges.

As a leader, your ability to manage stress and build resilience doesn't just benefit you; it sets a powerful example for your team. When you demonstrate calmness, focus, and a positive mindset, you create an environment where others feel supported and empowered to do their best work.

Incorporating these techniques into your leadership approach will help you navigate the complexities of leadership with grace and confidence. Whether you're leading a small team or a large organization, the skills of stress management and resilience will be invaluable in helping you achieve long-term success and personal fulfillment.

CRITICAL THINKING FOR LEADERS

As a leader, the ability to analyze situations objectively is crucial for making sound decisions, driving successful outcomes, and maintaining credibility with your team. Objective analysis involves removing personal biases, relying on accurate information, and making decisions based on evidence rather than assumptions. This guide will walk you through methods for achieving objectivity in your decision-making process, strategies for overcoming cognitive biases, gathering accurate information, and the benefits of evidence-based decision-making. We'll also provide real-world examples of how objective analysis has led to better leadership outcomes.

Understanding the Importance of Objective Analysis in Leadership

- ❖ Objective analysis is the foundation of effective leadership. It allows leaders to make decisions that are fair, well-informed, and aligned with the organization's goals. When leaders analyze situations objectively, they are better equipped to:
- ❖ Avoid making decisions based on emotions or incomplete information.

- Identify the root causes of problems rather than focusing on symptoms.
- Develop strategies that are realistic, achievable, and grounded in evidence.
- Build trust with their team by demonstrating fairness and transparency.

METHODS FOR ANALYZING SITUATIONS OBJECTIVELY

Clarify the Problem: The first step in objective analysis is to clearly define the problem or situation. This involves identifying the key issues at hand and understanding the context in which they exist. By clarifying the problem, you can avoid the common pitfall of addressing symptoms rather than the root cause.

Example: A leader in a manufacturing company notices a decline in product quality. Instead of assuming the issue is due to poor employee performance, the leader clarifies the problem by examining the entire production process. This leads to the discovery that outdated machinery is the root cause, not employee negligence.

Gather Accurate Information: Objective analysis requires access to accurate, relevant information. This involves collecting data from reliable sources, seeking input from various stakeholders, and ensuring that the information is up-to-date. Leaders should be wary of relying solely on anecdotal evidence or assumptions.

Example: A retail manager facing declining sales gathers information from sales reports, customer feedback, and market trends. By analyzing this data, the manager identifies that the decline is due to a shift in consumer preferences rather than poor customer service, allowing the manager to adjust the product offerings accordingly.

Break down the Situation: Breaking down a complex situation into smaller, more manageable parts can help you analyze it more effectively. This involves identifying the key components of the situation, understanding how they interact, and considering the potential impact of each component on the overall outcome.

Example: A leader in a nonprofit organization is tasked with improving volunteer engagement. Instead of tackling the issue as a whole, the leader breaks it down into factors such as communication, volunteer recognition, and scheduling flexibility. By addressing each factor individually, the leader is able to develop a comprehensive plan that improves engagement across the board.

Consider Multiple Perspectives: To analyze a situation objectively, it's important to consider multiple perspectives. This involves seeking input from different stakeholders, considering alternative viewpoints, and challenging your own assumptions. By doing so, you can gain a more complete understanding of the situation and avoid the trap of confirmation bias.

Example: A school principal is facing resistance from teachers regarding a new curriculum. Instead of dismissing the teachers' concerns, the principal seeks their input, considers their perspectives, and engages in open dialogue. This leads to a compromise that addresses the teachers' concerns while still achieving the curriculum's goals.

Overcoming Cognitive Biases in Decision-Making

Cognitive biases are systematic errors in thinking that can cloud judgment and lead to poor decision-making. As a leader, it's essential to recognize and overcome these biases to ensure that your decisions are objective and well-founded.

Confirmation Bias: Confirmation bias occurs when individuals favor information that confirms their existing beliefs and ignore information that contradicts them. To overcome this bias, actively seek out information that challenges your assumptions and be open to changing your perspective based on new evidence.

Example: A CEO believes that a particular marketing strategy is the key to success. To avoid confirmation bias, the CEO reviews data from previous campaigns, considers alternative strategies, and seeks input from the marketing team before making a decision.

Anchoring Bias: Anchoring bias occurs when individuals rely too heavily on the first piece of information they receive (the "anchor") when making decisions. To counter this bias, consider a wide range of information and avoid making decisions based solely on initial impressions.

Example: During salary negotiations, a manager avoids anchoring bias by considering the employee's experience, market rates, and the company's budget rather than focusing solely on the employee's initial salary request.

Availability Heuristic: The availability heuristic is a cognitive bias that causes individuals to overestimate the likelihood of events based on how easily they can recall similar instances. To mitigate this bias, rely on objective data and statistics rather than anecdotal evidence.

Example: A leader deciding whether to expand into a new market avoids the availability heuristic by conducting thorough market research and analyzing industry trends rather than relying on recent news stories about similar expansions.

Overconfidence Bias: Overconfidence bias occurs when individuals overestimate their knowledge, abilities, or the accuracy of their predictions. To combat this bias, regularly seek feedback, acknowledge uncertainties, and consider the possibility of being wrong.

Example: A project manager avoids overconfidence bias by involving team members in the planning process, seeking input from experts, and conducting risk assessments before committing to project timelines.

Making Decisions Based on Evidence

Evidence-based decision-making involves using data, research, and factual information to guide your decisions. This approach reduces the influence of personal biases and ensures that decisions are grounded in reality.

Use Data and Analytics: Collecting and analyzing data is a key component of evidence-based decision-making. This involves gathering quantitative and qualitative data relevant to the situation, analyzing trends, and using statistical methods to draw conclusions.

Example: A leader at a tech company uses customer usage data to make decisions about product development. By analyzing user behavior and feedback, the leader identifies which features are most valued by customers and prioritizes those in the development roadmap.

Consult Research and Best Practices: Consulting existing research and best practices can provide valuable insights and help inform your decisions. This involves reviewing academic studies, industry reports, and case studies to understand what has worked well in similar situations.

Example: A healthcare administrator looking to improve patient satisfaction reviews studies on patient-centered care, consults best practices from leading hospitals, and implements evidence-based strategies such as improving communication and reducing wait times.

Seek Expert Opinions: In complex situations, seeking the opinions of experts in the field can provide additional perspectives and help you make informed decisions. Experts can offer insights based on their experience, knowledge, and understanding of the subject matter.

Example: A financial leader facing a major investment decision consults with economists, financial analysts, and industry experts to gain a deeper understanding of market trends and risks before making the final decision.

Pilot Testing and Iterative Feedback: When implementing new strategies or initiatives, pilot testing and iterative feedback can provide real-world evidence of effectiveness. This involves testing a solution on a small scale, gathering feedback, and making adjustments before full implementation.

Example: A retail chain considering a new store layout tests the concept in a few locations, collects customer feedback, and analyzes sales data before rolling it out across all stores. This evidence-based approach ensures that the new layout meets customer needs and enhances the shopping experience.

The Benefits of Objective Analysis in Leadership

Objective analysis leads to better leadership outcomes in several ways:

Improved Decision-Making: By analyzing situations objectively, leaders make more informed decisions that are based on facts rather than assumptions. This reduces the risk of costly mistakes and ensures that decisions align with organizational goals.

Example: A leader who objectively analyzes market trends before launching a new product is more likely to succeed than one who relies on gut feelings or anecdotal evidence.

Enhanced Credibility: Leaders who consistently make objective, evidence-based decisions build credibility with their team, peers, and superiors. This credibility fosters trust and respect, which are essential for effective leadership.

Example: A leader who transparently shares the data and rationale behind their decisions earns the trust of their team, leading to greater buy-in and support for initiatives.

Increased Innovation: Objective analysis encourages leaders to consider new ideas and approaches, rather than sticking to the status quo. By challenging assumptions and seeking out diverse perspectives, leaders can drive innovation and find creative solutions to problems.

Example: A leader in a tech company uses objective analysis to explore emerging technologies and trends. By considering new possibilities and being open to change, the leader drives innovation and keeps the company competitive.

Better Risk Management: Objective analysis helps leaders identify and mitigate risks by considering all relevant factors and potential outcomes. This proactive approach to risk management reduces the likelihood of unexpected challenges and enhances the organization's resilience.

Example: A leader overseeing a major project uses objective analysis to assess potential risks, such as supply chain disruptions or regulatory changes. By planning for these risks in advance, the leader ensures that the project stays on track and within budget.

Real-World Examples of Objective Analysis Leading to Successful Outcomes

Example 1: IBM's Shift to Cloud Computing: In the early 2000s, IBM faced declining sales in its traditional hardware business. Rather than relying on past successes, IBM's leadership objectively analyzed market trends and identified cloud computing as a key growth area. By gathering data, consulting experts, and making evidence-based decisions, IBM successfully transitioned to a services-oriented business model, becoming a leader in cloud computing in the early 2000s, IBM faced a decline in its traditional hardware business. Instead of relying on past successes, IBM's leadership objectively analyzed market trends and identified cloud computing as a key growth area. By gathering data, consulting experts, and making evidence-based decisions, IBM successfully transitioned to a services-oriented business model, becoming a leader in cloud computing.

Example 2: Toyota's Kaizen Approach: Toyota's commitment to continuous improvement, known as the Kaizen approach, is a prime example of objective analysis in action. Toyota encourages employees at all levels to identify areas for improvement and to base decisions on data and facts. This culture of objective analysis has led to significant innovations in manufacturing processes, improved product quality, and enhanced efficiency, making Toyota one of the most successful automakers in the world.

Example 3: Google's Data-Driven HR Decisions: Google is known for its data-driven approach to decision-making, including in human resources. The company uses data and analytics to inform decisions about hiring, employee development, and workplace policies. For example, Google's analysis of employee performance data led to the creation of Project Oxygen, which identified key behaviors that make managers effective. This evidence-based approach has helped Google create a high-performing work environment and retain top talent.

DECISION-MAKING WITHOUT FORMAL AUTHORITY

In any organization, the ability to make effective decisions is crucial for driving success. However, making decisions without formal authority presents unique challenges. It requires a careful balance of risk management, input from others, and confidence in your decisions. This framework is designed to help you navigate these challenges and make impactful decisions even when you lack formal authority.

Understanding the Role of Influence in Decision-Making

When you don't have formal authority, your ability to influence others becomes your most valuable asset. Influence is built through relationships, expertise, and trust. Before making decisions, focus on building a strong foundation of influence by demonstrating your knowledge, reliability, and commitment to the organization's goals. This groundwork will make it easier to gain support for your decisions and ensure that others take your recommendations seriously.

Step 1: Clarify the Decision at Hand

The first step in making an effective decision is to clearly define the problem or opportunity. Understanding the scope and implications of the decision is critical. Ask yourself the following questions:

- ❖ What exactly needs to be decided?
- ❖ What are the potential outcomes of this decision?
- ❖ Who will be affected by this decision?

By answering these questions, you can ensure that you are addressing the right issue and that your decision-making process is focused on the most relevant factors.

Example:

A team leader in a marketing department is tasked with improving the company's social media presence. Without formal authority, the leader must first clarify the specific goals of the initiative—whether it's increasing followers, boosting engagement, or driving sales. By clearly defining the decision, the leader can focus on the most effective strategies.

Step 2: Gather Relevant Information

Effective decision-making relies on accurate, comprehensive information. Without formal authority, it's especially important to gather data and insights from various sources to build a strong case for your decision.

Conduct Research: Look at industry trends, best practices, and case studies relevant to the decision.

Seek Input from Others: Engage with colleagues, stakeholders, and experts to gather different perspectives and gain a deeper understanding of the issue.

Analyze Data: Use data to back up your decision, whether it's customer feedback, sales figures, or market analysis.

Example:
A project manager without direct authority over team members needs to decide on a new project management tool. The manager gathers input from team members about their pain points with the current system, researches the most popular tools in the industry, and analyzes the cost-benefit of each option. By compiling this information, the manager can make an informed recommendation.

Step 3: Evaluate the Risks and Benefits

Every decision involves some level of risk. As a leader without formal authority, it's crucial to assess these risks carefully and balance them against the potential benefits. Consider the following:

Identify Potential Risks: What could go wrong if the decision is implemented? How likely are these risks, and what impact would they have?

Assess the Benefits: What are the potential positive outcomes? How will this decision contribute to the organization's goals?

Develop Contingency Plans: Consider what steps you can take to mitigate risks if they materialize.

Example:

A middle manager wants to propose a new customer service strategy that involves significant changes to existing processes. The manager evaluates the risks, such as potential resistance from staff and the initial cost of implementation, against the benefits, including improved customer satisfaction and long-term cost savings. By weighing these factors, the manager can present a well-rounded proposal.

Step 4: Seek Input and Build Consensus

One of the most important aspects of decision-making without formal authority is building consensus. This involves bringing others on board with your decision by seeking their input and addressing their concerns.

Engage Stakeholders: Identify key stakeholders who will be affected by the decision or who have influence over its implementation. Involve them early in the decision-making process to ensure their support.

Communicate Transparently: Clearly explain the rationale behind your decision, using the information and data you've gathered. Be open to feedback and willing to adjust your approach based on input from others.

Address Concerns: Listen to any concerns or objections and address them thoughtfully. Show that you've considered different perspectives and are making a decision that is in the best interest of the organization.

Example:

A department head without direct control over the company's budget wants to introduce a new training program. The department head seeks input from other department heads, HR, and the finance team to ensure the program aligns with company priorities and budget constraints. By involving these stakeholders in the decision-making process, the department head builds consensus and secures the necessary support for the initiative.

Step 5: Assert the Decision with Confidence

Once you've gathered input and built consensus, it's time to assert the decision confidently. Asserting a decision without formal authority requires a blend of confidence and diplomacy.

Here's how to do it:

Present the Decision Clearly: Clearly communicate the decision, along with the rationale and evidence that supports it. Use data and real-world examples to back up your points.

Show Confidence: Display confidence in your decision by speaking with conviction and demonstrating your expertise. Confidence is contagious—when you believe in the decision, others are more likely to believe in it too.

Be Prepared to Defend the Decision: Anticipate potential objections and be ready to address them. Having a well-thought-out rationale will help you respond effectively to any challenges.

Example:
A sales manager without the authority to make pricing decisions identifies an opportunity to offer a temporary discount to boost sales. After gathering data on competitor pricing and customer demand, the manager confidently presents the proposal to senior leadership, highlighting the potential for increased market share. The manager's confidence and thorough preparation lead to the approval of the discount strategy.

Step 6: Monitor and Adapt

After the decision has been made and implemented, it's essential to monitor its impact and be ready to adapt if necessary. This ongoing process ensures that the decision continues to serve the organization's goals and allows for adjustments in response to new information or changing circumstances.

Track Key Metrics: Identify key performance indicators (KPIs) that will help you measure the success of the decision. Regularly review these metrics to assess whether the decision is achieving the desired outcomes.

Solicit Feedback: Continue to seek feedback from stakeholders and team members to understand how the decision is impacting them. Be open to making adjustments based on this feedback.

Be Flexible: If the decision isn't delivering the expected results, be willing to pivot and explore alternative solutions. Flexibility is key to maintaining effectiveness in a dynamic environment.

Example:

A leader in a nonprofit organization makes a decision to launch a new fundraising campaign without formal authority over the marketing team. After the campaign is launched, the leader monitors donation levels, analyzes the effectiveness of different marketing channels, and seeks feedback from donors. When initial results show that certain tactics aren't working as expected, the leader adjusts the campaign strategy to focus on more successful approaches.

Real-Life Scenarios of Decision-Making without Formal Authority

Scenario 1: Leading Cross-Functional Projects A mid-level manager at a tech company is tasked with leading a cross-functional project to develop a new software feature. The manager has no formal authority over the team members from different departments, but by building strong relationships, gathering input from each department, and presenting a clear plan, the manager successfully leads the project to completion. The key to success was the manager's ability to balance the needs of different departments, assert decisions confidently, and adapt to challenges as they arose.

Scenario 2: Introducing Process Improvements An operations supervisor in a manufacturing plant identifies inefficiencies in the production process. Without formal authority to implement changes, the supervisor gathers data on the inefficiencies, seeks input from frontline workers, and presents a well-supported proposal to senior management. The proposal is accepted, leading to a significant improvement in production efficiency. The supervisor's success was rooted in their ability to make data-driven decisions, involve stakeholders in the process, and communicate the benefits of the proposed changes effectively.

Scenario 3: Managing Organizational Change A human resources specialist at a large corporation is passionate about improving employee engagement. Despite not having the authority to mandate changes, the specialist conducts surveys to gather input from employees, researches best practices in employee engagement, and collaborates with department heads to develop an engagement strategy. By presenting a compelling case and gaining buy-in from leadership, the specialist successfully implements the strategy, resulting in higher employee satisfaction and retention rates. The specialist's ability to gather evidence, build consensus, and assert the decision with confidence was critical to the initiative's success.

PART III: LEADING AND INSPIRING TEAMS

MOTIVATING AND GUIDING TEAMS WITHOUT A TITLE

In today's dynamic work environments, effective teamwork is essential for achieving organizational goals. However, leading a team without a formal title can present unique challenges. As a team-building expert, I will outline techniques for fostering collaboration within teams, focusing on strategies that encourage open communication, shared goals, and mutual respect. These strategies are particularly valuable for those who lead by influence rather than authority, as they emphasize the power of building strong, cooperative relationships. By implementing these techniques, leaders can enhance team performance and create a positive, collaborative work environment.

TECHNIQUES FOR FOSTERING TEAM COLLABORATION

Collaboration is the cornerstone of successful teamwork. It involves working together towards common goals, leveraging diverse skills and perspectives, and creating a cohesive unit that can tackle complex challenges. In a collaborative team, members feel valued, engaged, and motivated to contribute their best efforts. This not only improves individual performance but also drives overall team success.

For leaders without formal titles, fostering collaboration is key to gaining influence and driving positive outcomes. By encouraging a collaborative culture, these leaders can build trust, inspire creativity, and ensure that everyone is working towards the same objectives.

Encouraging Open Communication

Open communication is fundamental to collaboration. It allows team members to share ideas, voice concerns, and provide feedback, creating an environment where everyone feels heard and respected. For leaders without formal authority, facilitating open communication is a powerful way to build credibility and influence.

1. Create a Safe Space for Dialogue

One of the most important aspects of fostering open communication is creating a safe space where team members feel comfortable expressing their thoughts and opinions. This involves establishing an atmosphere of trust, where individuals are not afraid of judgment or repercussions for speaking up.

Example:

A team member hesitates to share a new idea during meetings because they fear it might be dismissed. The leader, recognizing this hesitation, addresses the entire team, emphasizing the importance of diverse perspectives and encouraging everyone to contribute without fear. Over time, this approach fosters a more open and inclusive environment, leading to increased innovation and collaboration.

2. Practice Active Listening

Active listening is a critical skill for any leader, especially those without formal authority. It involves fully engaging with the speaker, understanding their message, and responding thoughtfully. By practicing active listening, leaders can demonstrate that they value team members' input, which in turn encourages more open communication.

Example:

During a team meeting, a leader without a formal title notices that a team member seems disengaged. The leader approaches them afterward and asks for their thoughts on the discussion. By actively listening to the team member's concerns, the leader not only addresses potential issues but also strengthens the team member's trust and willingness to communicate openly in the future.

3. Facilitate Regular Check-Ins

Regular check-ins are an effective way to maintain open communication within a team. These can be one-on-one meetings, team huddles, or informal conversations where team members can discuss their progress, challenges, and any concerns they might have.

Example:

A project team is working under tight deadlines, and stress levels are high. The leader schedules weekly check-ins with each team member to gauge their workload, offer support, and address any issues before they escalate. This proactive approach helps prevent misunderstandings and keeps communication channels open.

Promoting Shared Goals

Shared goals unify a team and provide a clear direction for their efforts. When team members are aligned with common objectives, collaboration becomes more natural and focused. Leaders without formal authority can play a crucial role in promoting shared goals by ensuring that everyone understands the purpose of their work and how it contributes to the bigger picture.

1. Clarify the Team's Mission and Objectives

A clear understanding of the team's mission and objectives is essential for fostering collaboration. Leaders should communicate these goals effectively and ensure that each team member understands how their role contributes to achieving them.

Example:

In a marketing team, the leader without formal authority takes the initiative to create a visual roadmap that outlines the team's objectives for the upcoming quarter. This roadmap is shared with the entire team, providing a clear and tangible representation of what they are working towards. As a result, team members are more motivated and aligned in their efforts.

2. Involve the Team in Goal Setting

Involving team members in the goal-setting process increases their commitment to achieving those goals. When individuals have a say in setting objectives, they are more likely to take ownership and collaborate with others to reach them.

Example:

A software development team is tasked with delivering a new product feature. The leader facilitates a brainstorming session where team members can suggest milestones, deadlines, and success metrics. By involving the team in this process, the leader fosters a sense of ownership and encourages collaboration towards a shared outcome.

3. Align Individual Goals with Team Goals

For collaboration to be effective, individual goals must be aligned with team goals. Leaders can help team members understand how their personal objectives fit into the broader team mission, creating a sense of purpose and direction.

Example:

A sales team is working towards an ambitious quarterly target. The leader meets with each team member to discuss their individual sales goals and how these contribute to the overall target. By aligning personal and team goals, the leader ensures that everyone is working towards the same objectives and feels motivated to collaborate.

Building Mutual Respect

Mutual respect is a fundamental component of any successful team. It fosters a positive work environment where team members feel valued and appreciated, which in turn enhances collaboration. Leaders without formal authority can cultivate mutual respect by modeling respectful behavior and encouraging others to do the same.

1. Lead by Example

Leaders set the tone for how team members interact with each other. By consistently demonstrating respect, empathy, and fairness, leaders can create a culture of mutual respect within the team.

Example:

In a cross-functional team, the leader without formal authority makes a point of acknowledging the contributions of each team member, regardless of their role or seniority. This behavior encourages others to do the same, fostering an environment where everyone feels respected and valued.

2. Address Disrespectful Behavior Promptly

Disrespectful behavior can quickly erode trust and collaboration within a team. Leaders must address any instances of disrespect promptly and constructively, ensuring that they do not escalate or become normalized.

Example:

During a team meeting, a member dismisses another's idea in a rude manner. The leader immediately intervenes, reminding the team of the importance of respectful communication. The leader then follows up with both individuals privately to ensure that the issue is resolved and that similar behavior does not occur in the future.

3. Encourage Peer Recognition

Encouraging peer recognition is a powerful way to build mutual respect within a team. When team members recognize each other's contributions, it strengthens their relationships and promotes a collaborative atmosphere.

Example:

In a customer service team, the leader introduces a "shout-out" board where team members can post notes of appreciation for their colleagues' efforts. This simple initiative boosts morale, encourages teamwork, and reinforces the value of mutual respect.

Strategies for Fostering Collaboration without a Formal Title

Leading without a formal title requires a unique approach to fostering collaboration. The following strategies are designed to help leaders build strong, cooperative teams, even when they lack formal authority.

1. Build Strong Relationships

Strong relationships are the foundation of effective collaboration. Leaders without formal authority should focus on building trust, rapport, and mutual respect with each team member. This involves taking the time to understand their strengths, challenges, and motivations.

Example:

A team leader in a remote work environment makes an effort to connect with team members on a personal level through regular video calls and informal chats. By building strong relationships, the leader fosters a sense of camaraderie and collaboration, despite the physical distance.

2. Empower Team Members

Empowering team members involves giving them the autonomy to make decisions, take ownership of their work, and contribute to the team's success. When individuals feel empowered, they are more likely to collaborate and support each other.

Example:

A project coordinator without formal authority encourages

team members to take the lead on specific tasks within a project. By giving them the autonomy to make decisions and solve problems, the coordinator fosters a collaborative environment where everyone feels invested in the outcome.

3. Facilitate Collaboration Tools and Practices

Providing the right tools and practices can significantly enhance collaboration within a team. Leaders should identify and implement tools that facilitate communication, project management, and information sharing.

Example:

A leader in a creative agency introduces a collaboration tool that allows team members to share ideas, provide feedback, and track progress in real-time. This tool streamlines communication and ensures that everyone is on the same page, leading to more effective collaboration.

4. Promote a Collaborative Mindset

A collaborative mindset is one where team members see themselves as part of a larger whole, working together towards a common goal. Leaders can promote this mindset by encouraging teamwork, recognizing collaborative efforts, and reinforcing the value of collective success.

Example:

In a product development team, the leader emphasizes the importance of collaboration by celebrating team achievements rather than individual accomplishments. This approach encourages team members to work together and prioritize the success of the team over personal recognition.

5. Encourage Diversity of Thought

Diversity of thought brings different perspectives, ideas, and approaches to the table, which can enhance creativity and problem-solving within a team. Leaders should encourage team members to share their unique perspectives and consider alternative viewpoints.

Example:

During a strategy meeting, the leader encourages team members from different departments to share their insights on a new project. By valuing diverse perspectives, the leader fosters a more inclusive and collaborative environment, leading to innovative solutions.

Real-Life Examples of Successful Collaboration Without Formal Authority

The Google X Team: Google X, the company's innovation lab, is known for its collaborative approach to developing groundbreaking technologies. The team operates with a flat structure, where formal titles are less important than the ability to contribute ideas and work together. By fostering an environment of open communication and mutual respect, Google X has been able to innovate and create successful products like self-driving cars and smart contact lenses.

Pixar's Braintrust Meetings: Pixar's Braintrust meetings are a prime example of collaboration without formal authority. These meetings bring together directors, writers, and other key creatives to discuss the progress of a film. There are no formal titles or hierarchies in these meetings—everyone's input is valued equally. This collaborative approach has led to the creation of some of the most successful animated films in history.

The Apollo 13 Mission: The successful return of the Apollo 13 mission is often attributed to the collaborative efforts of NASA's engineers and astronauts, many of whom did not have formal authority over the mission. Faced with a life-threatening situation, the team worked together to devise a solution, leveraging their collective expertise and creativity. This example demonstrates the power of collaboration, even in the absence of formal titles.

ENCOURAGING INITIATIVE AND ACCOUNTABILITY

As a leadership trainer, fostering a culture of initiative and accountability within teams is essential, especially when you're not in a position of formal authority. Without the power to dictate actions, you must rely on influence, trust, and the strategic creation of an environment where team members feel empowered to take ownership of their tasks and responsibilities. In this guide, I will outline methods for encouraging initiative and accountability among team members, offering practical tips and real-world examples that highlight the effectiveness of these strategies.

The Importance of Initiative and Accountability

Initiative refers to the willingness of team members to take action independently, without waiting for explicit instructions. Accountability, on the other hand, is the sense of responsibility individuals feel for their actions and their outcomes. Both are critical components of a high-performing team. When team members are proactive and hold themselves accountable, the team becomes more agile, innovative, and capable of achieving its goals.

Creating a Culture of Ownership and Responsibility

Fostering a culture of ownership and responsibility starts with creating an environment where team members feel valued, trusted, and empowered. This involves several key strategies that can be implemented even when you don't have formal authority.

1. Lead by Example

Even without formal authority, your behavior sets the tone for the rest of the team. Demonstrating initiative and holding yourself accountable for your actions encourages others to do the same. By consistently modeling the behavior you wish to see in your team, you create a standard that others are likely to follow.

Case Study: A Marketing Team's Turnaround

In a marketing team facing declining performance, a mid-level team member began taking the initiative by volunteering to lead new projects and consistently meeting deadlines. Despite not being the official team leader, their actions inspired others to step up, leading to a noticeable improvement in the teams overall productivity and morale. This individual's commitment to accountability and initiative set a powerful example that transformed the team's dynamics.

2. Foster a Trusting Environment

Trust is the foundation of any successful team. When team members trust each other, they are more likely to take risks, share ideas, and take ownership of their work. Building trust involves being transparent, honest, and consistent in your actions and communication.

Practical Tip: Encourage open communication by regularly checking in with team members, listening to their concerns, and providing constructive feedback. This not only builds trust but also shows that you value their input and are invested in their success.

Success Story: Building Trust in a Cross-Functional Team

In a cross-functional team working on a complex project, initial progress was slow due to a lack of trust and collaboration. By initiating regular team-building activities and promoting open dialogue, the project manager (who did not have formal authority over all team members) gradually built trust within the team. As trust grew, team members became more willing to take ownership of their tasks, leading to faster decision-making and improved project outcomes.

3. Encourage Autonomy and Empowerment

Autonomy is crucial for fostering initiative. When team members feel they have control over their work, they are more likely to take the initiative to improve processes, solve problems, and contribute to the team's success. Empowerment involves giving team members the authority and resources they need to take ownership of their work.

Practical Tip: Delegate tasks and responsibilities, allowing team members to make decisions and solve problems independently. Provide guidance and support when needed, but avoid micromanaging.

Case Study: Empowering Team Members in a Software Development Project

In a software development project, the team leader encouraged developers to take ownership of their respective modules. By empowering them to make design decisions and experiment with new technologies, the leader fostered a sense of ownership and pride in their work. This approach not only accelerated the project's progress but also led to innovative solutions that exceeded the client's expectations.

4. Set Clear Expectations and Goals

Clear expectations and goals provide a roadmap for team members, helping them understand what is expected of them and how their work contributes to the team's overall success. When team members know what they need to achieve, they are more likely to take the initiative to meet those expectations.

Practical Tip: Involve team members in the goal-setting process to increase their commitment and ownership. Clearly communicate the objectives, deadlines, and criteria for success, and ensure that everyone understands their role in achieving the goals.

Success Story: A Sales Team's Journey to Exceeding Targets

In a sales team struggling to meet its quarterly targets, the team leader organized a goal-setting workshop where team members could contribute to setting realistic and achievable sales targets. By involving the team in the process, the leader increased their commitment to achieving the targets. The team not only met but exceeded its goals, with each member taking responsibility for their individual and collective performance.

5. Provide Feedback and Recognition

Feedback and recognition are powerful tools for reinforcing initiative and accountability. Regular feedback helps team members understand how they are performing and where they can improve, while recognition reinforces positive behavior and motivates others to follow suit.

Practical Tip: Implement a system of regular feedback sessions where team members can receive constructive criticism and praise for their work. Recognize and celebrate individual and team achievements publicly to encourage a culture of accountability and initiative.

Case Study: Enhancing Performance through Feedback in a Customer Service Team

A customer service team was experiencing low morale and high turnover due to a lack of feedback and recognition. The team leader introduced weekly feedback sessions where team members could discuss their performance, challenges, and successes. By providing constructive feedback and recognizing outstanding performance, the leader improved the team's morale and accountability. This led to better customer service outcomes and a more engaged and motivated team.

6. Encourage Risk-Taking and Innovation

Encouraging team members to take risks and innovate is essential for fostering initiative. When team members feel safe to experiment and explore new ideas, they are more likely to take the initiative to drive change and improvement within the team.

Practical Tip: Create an environment where failure is seen as a learning opportunity rather than a setback. Encourage team members to experiment with new approaches and support them when things don't go as planned.

Success Story: Driving Innovation in a Product Development Team

In a product development team, the leader encouraged team members to explore new technologies and approaches to solve complex problems. By creating a culture that valued innovation and supported risk-taking, the leader enabled the team to develop groundbreaking products that set the company apart from its competitors.

Practical Tips for Creating a Culture of Ownership and Responsibility

Creating a culture of ownership and responsibility within a team requires consistent effort and strategic actions. Here are some practical tips to help you foster this culture, even when you're not in charge:

Communicate the Bigger Picture: Help team members understand how their work contributes to the team's overall goals and the organization's success. When individuals see the impact of their efforts, they are more likely to take ownership and responsibility for their work.

Encourage Collaboration and Teamwork: Foster a collaborative environment where team members feel supported by their peers. Encourage them to share ideas, collaborate on projects, and hold each other accountable for meeting team objectives.

Create Opportunities for Leadership: Provide team members with opportunities to take on leadership roles within the team, such as leading a project or organizing a team event. This not only encourages initiative but also helps individuals develop their leadership skills.

Promote Continuous Learning: Encourage team members to continuously develop their skills and knowledge. Provide access to training, workshops, and other resources that support their professional growth. A culture of learning fosters initiative and a sense of responsibility for personal and team development.

Establish Accountability Mechanisms: Implement mechanisms that hold team members accountable for their work, such as regular progress reports, performance reviews, and peer evaluations. Ensure that these mechanisms are fair, transparent, and focused on growth and improvement.

BUILDING TRUST AND RESPECT AMONG PEERS

In the professional world, leadership is not solely defined by a title or position. Often, individuals find themselves in situations where they need to lead, influence, or guide others without holding a formal leadership role. In these cases, the ability to establish credibility and gain respect from peers becomes crucial. As a leadership mentor, I will outline the key qualities that can help you build credibility and respect within a team, and I will provide examples of how expertise, reliability, and integrity play a vital role in effective leadership from within.

ESTABLISHING CREDIBILITY IN NON-LEADERSHIP ROLES

The Importance of Expertise

Expertise is one of the most significant factors in establishing credibility. When you demonstrate a deep understanding of your field, peers naturally begin to respect your knowledge and opinions. Expertise does not just mean having a technical grasp of the subject matter; it also involves the ability to apply knowledge practically and effectively in real-world scenarios.

Building Expertise

To establish expertise, you must commit to continuous learning and staying updated with the latest developments in your field. This can involve formal education, attending workshops, engaging in professional networks, and being an avid reader of industry literature. Moreover, practical experience is invaluable. The more you apply what you know, the more nuanced and informed your expertise will become.

Example: Expertise in Action

Consider the example of Sarah, a software developer on a team tasked with developing a new product. Although Sarah was not the team leader, she had extensive knowledge of the specific programming language the team was using. Her deep understanding allowed her to troubleshoot complex issues that others struggled with. By consistently offering solutions and providing insights that advanced the project, Sarah earned the respect of her peers. Her expertise became a cornerstone of the team's success, and she naturally assumed a leadership role within the group, guiding decisions and mentoring less experienced team members.

Reliability as a Pillar of Credibility

Reliability is another critical component in gaining respect from peers. When you consistently deliver high-quality work on time and meet your commitments, others begin to trust you. Reliability is about being dependable and showing that you can be counted on, no matter the circumstances.

Demonstrating Reliability

To be seen as reliable, you should focus on consistency in your actions. This includes meeting deadlines, being punctual for meetings, and following through on promises. Additionally, effective communication is key. If you encounter obstacles that might prevent you from delivering as promised, it's essential to communicate these issues promptly and work with your team to find solutions.

Example: Reliability in Action

John, a project coordinator, was known for his meticulous attention to detail and his ability to deliver projects on time. Even though he didn't hold a managerial position, his team often relied on him to keep projects on track. When faced with a particularly challenging deadline, John proactively identified potential bottlenecks and reallocated resources to ensure the team met its objectives. His consistent reliability earned him the trust and respect of his peers, and they often looked to him for guidance on how to manage their own tasks more effectively.

Integrity: The Foundation of Trust and Respect

Integrity is perhaps the most crucial quality for anyone looking to lead from within. Integrity means being honest, ethical, and transparent in all your actions. It involves sticking to your principles, even when it's difficult, and ensuring that your actions align with your words.

Living with Integrity

To cultivate integrity, you must commit to being truthful and ethical in all your interactions. This includes owning up to mistakes, giving credit where it's due, and treating everyone with respect. Integrity also involves being transparent about your intentions and decisions, which helps build trust among your peers.

Example: Integrity in Action

Emma, a financial analyst, was part of a team working on a high-stakes project. During the project, she discovered a significant error in the financial data that could have impacted the entire project's outcome. Although correcting the mistake would delay the project, Emma chose to bring it to the team's attention immediately. Her honesty, even in the face of potential backlash, solidified her reputation as someone who could be trusted to do the right thing, even when it was difficult. Over time, Emma's integrity became a hallmark of her leadership style, and colleagues regularly sought her advice on ethical dilemmas.

Building Relationships through Effective Communication

While expertise, reliability, and integrity are foundational qualities, **effective communication** is the glue that binds them together. How you communicate with your peers can significantly impact your ability to establish credibility and gain respect.

Practicing Effective Communication

Effective communication involves active listening, being clear and concise in your messages, and adapting your communication style to suit the needs of your audience. It also means being approachable and open to feedback, which helps build stronger relationships with your peers.

Example: Communication in Action

Michael, a mid-level engineer, was known for his ability to explain complex technical concepts in a way that was easy to understand. When his team faced challenges, he would facilitate discussions, ensuring that everyone had a chance to voice their opinions. His clear and inclusive communication style made team members feel valued and respected, and as a result, they were more willing to follow his lead, even though he wasn't their formal supervisor.

Leveraging Networking and Collaboration

In addition to personal qualities, **networking** and **collaboration** play crucial roles in establishing credibility and gaining respect. Building a strong network of professional relationships allows you to share knowledge, gain insights, and provide support to others, which in turn enhances your credibility.

Building a Strong Network

To build a strong network, actively seek out opportunities to collaborate with others, both within and outside your immediate team. Attend industry events, join professional organizations, and engage in online communities relevant to your field. Networking is not just about what you can gain but also about how you can contribute to others' success.

Example: Networking and Collaboration in Action

Lisa, a graphic designer, made it a point to attend industry conferences and participate in online design forums. Through these activities, she built a robust network of contacts who provided her with fresh perspectives and feedback on her work. When her team needed to rebrand a major client's image, Lisa leveraged her network to gather insights and collaborate with experts in branding. Her ability to bring in external expertise not only improved the project's outcome but also demonstrated her value to the team, earning her respect and recognition.

Navigating Challenges with Diplomacy

Finally, **diplomacy** is an essential skill for anyone leading from within. Navigating conflicts, addressing disagreements, and managing difficult situations require a diplomatic approach that balances assertiveness with empathy.

Practicing Diplomacy

To be diplomatic, focus on understanding others' perspectives and finding common ground. When conflicts arise, address them calmly and constructively, seeking solutions that benefit the entire team. Avoid taking sides or engaging in office politics, as this can undermine your credibility.

Example: Diplomacy in Action

When a dispute arose between two departments over resource allocation, Kevin, a team member with no formal leadership role, stepped in to mediate. He organized a meeting where both sides could express their concerns and worked to identify a solution that met everyone's needs. Kevin's diplomatic approach not only resolved the conflict but also strengthened relationships between the departments. His peers recognized his ability to manage difficult situations, and he gained respect for his leadership skills.

The Long-Term Impact of Building Credibility and Respect

Establishing credibility and gaining respect without holding a formal leadership position is not just about achieving short-term goals. It's about building a long-term reputation as someone who can be trusted, relied upon, and looked up to within the organization. Over time, these qualities can open doors to new opportunities, whether it's a promotion, a leadership role, or simply greater influence within your team.

The Ripple Effect of Credibility

When you establish credibility, it has a ripple effect. Others in the organization notice your expertise, reliability, and integrity, and this can lead to increased responsibilities and recognition.

Even without a formal title, you become a leader in the eyes of your peers, someone they turn to for guidance and support.

Example: The Long-Term Impact

Consider the story of Mark, a project manager who consistently demonstrated expertise, reliability, and integrity over several years. Although he was not in an executive position, his reputation for getting things done and leading by example led to his involvement in high-profile projects and strategic decision-making processes. Eventually, Mark was promoted to a leadership role, not because of his title, but because of the credibility and respect he had earned from his peers and superiors.

HANDLING CONFLICTS WITH DIPLOMACY

In any workplace, conflicts are inevitable. They can arise from differences in opinions, misunderstandings, or competing interests. Handling conflicts with diplomacy, especially when you're not in a leadership position, is a crucial skill that can help maintain positive relationships, foster a collaborative environment, and ensure that the team remains focused on its goals. This guide will explore techniques for de-escalating tensions, finding common ground, and maintaining positive relationships. By using real-world examples, we will illustrate how these techniques can lead to successful conflict resolution, even when you don't hold formal authority.

The Importance of Diplomacy in Conflict Resolution

Diplomacy involves the art of managing relationships, negotiating, and communicating in a way that minimizes conflict and fosters cooperation. When you're not in a leadership position, using diplomacy to handle conflicts can prevent the situation from escalating and ensure that all parties feel heard and respected. Diplomatic conflict resolution is essential for maintaining team cohesion, which is critical for achieving collective goals.

De-Escalating Tensions

The first step in handling conflict is to de-escalate the situation. High tensions can lead to emotional responses, making it difficult to resolve the issue constructively. Here are some techniques to de-escalate tensions:

Stay Calm and Composed: When emotions run high, it's essential to remain calm and composed. Your demeanor can influence others, helping to lower the emotional temperature of the situation. Take deep breaths, speak slowly, and maintain a neutral tone.

Acknowledge the Other Person's Feelings: Validating the other person's feelings doesn't mean you agree with them, but it shows that you recognize their emotions. Phrases like "I can see that this is really frustrating for you" can help defuse anger and open the door to more rational discussions.

Pause and Reflect: If the conflict is becoming heated, suggest taking a short break. This gives everyone time to cool down and think about the issue more clearly. When you reconvene, the situation is likely to be less charged.

Example: De-Escalating Tensions in a Team Meeting

During a team meeting, two colleagues, Jane and Tom, began arguing over the best approach to a project. The discussion quickly became heated, with both raising their voices. As a peer without formal authority, you might say, "I think we're all really passionate about this project, and that's great. Let's take a five-minute break to gather our thoughts, and then we can come back and find a solution that works for everyone." This approach acknowledges their emotions, provides a cooling-off period, and sets the stage for a more productive conversation.

Finding Common Ground

Once tensions have been de-escalated, the next step is to find common ground. This involves identifying shared goals or values that both parties can agree on, which can serve as a foundation for resolving the conflict.

Identify Shared Interests: Start by identifying what both parties have in common. This could be a shared goal, such as completing a project on time, or a mutual desire for the team's success. By focusing on these shared interests, you can shift the conversation from a confrontational to a collaborative tone.

Reframe the Conflict: Reframing involves changing the way the conflict is perceived. Instead of viewing it as a win-lose situation, present it as a problem that both parties need to solve together. This encourages collaboration rather than competition.

Ask Open-Ended Questions: Open-ended questions encourage dialogue and can help uncover underlying concerns or needs that may not have been initially apparent. Questions like "What do you think is the most important outcome we need to achieve?" or "How do you see us working together to solve this issue?" can facilitate finding common ground.

Example: Finding Common Ground in a Cross-Departmental Conflict

Imagine you're working on a project that requires input from both the marketing and sales departments. A conflict arises because marketing wants to prioritize brand image, while sales is focused on immediate revenue generation. As a mediator, you could say, "It seems like both departments are committed to the company's success, but we're approaching it from different angles. What if we look at strategies that enhance our brand while also driving sales? How can we combine our strengths to achieve both objectives?" This reframing highlights the shared goal and encourages collaboration.

Maintaining Positive Relationships

Maintaining positive relationships during and after conflict resolution is vital for long-term team success. The way a conflict is handled can either strengthen or weaken relationships, so it's important to approach the situation with the goal of preserving or even improving interpersonal dynamics.

Communicate Respectfully: Throughout the conflict resolution process, ensure that you communicate respectfully. Avoid blame, sarcasm, or dismissive language. Instead, focus on using "I" statements, such as "I feel" or "I think," to express your perspective without attacking the other person.

Seek Win-Win Solutions: Aim for solutions that satisfy the needs of all parties involved. A win-win outcome is one where both sides feel that their concerns have been addressed and that they've gained something positive from the resolution.

Follow Up: After a conflict has been resolved, follow up with the parties involved to ensure that the solution is working and that there are no lingering issues. This demonstrates your commitment to maintaining positive relationships and shows that you value ongoing communication.

Example: Maintaining Positive Relationships after a Conflict

After resolving a disagreement between two team members about resource allocation, you might follow up by saying, "I'm glad we were able to come to an agreement on the resource allocation. How are things going with the new plan? Is there anything we need to adjust?" This follow-up shows that you're invested in the team's success and that you care about maintaining positive relationships.

Techniques for Diplomatic Conflict Resolution

To handle conflicts with diplomacy, especially when you're not in a leadership position, consider the following techniques:

Active Listening: Listen carefully to all parties involved in the conflict. Active listening involves not just hearing the words but understanding the emotions and intentions behind them. By showing that you genuinely care about what others are saying, you build trust and open the door to constructive dialogue.

Empathy: Put yourself in the other person's shoes. Understanding their perspective, even if you don't agree with it, can help you approach the conflict with compassion and find solutions that consider everyone's needs.

Neutral Language: Use neutral, non-confrontational language when addressing the conflict. Avoid words that could be perceived as accusatory or judgmental. Instead of saying, "You never listen to my ideas," try, "I feel like my ideas aren't being heard. Can we discuss how we can ensure everyone's contributions are considered?"

Focus on the Issue, Not the Person: Keep the discussion centered on the issue at hand, rather than personal attributes or behaviors. This prevents the conflict from becoming personal and helps maintain professional relationships.

Mediation: If the conflict is particularly complex or emotionally charged, consider bringing in a neutral third party to mediate the discussion. A mediator can help facilitate communication, ensure that both sides are heard, and guide the parties toward a resolution.

Example: Diplomatic Conflict Resolution in Action

Let's say two colleagues, Alex and Jamie, have a conflict over the direction of a project. Alex feels that Jamie is too focused on minor details, while Jamie thinks Alex is rushing the project without considering potential risks. As a peer, you might use diplomatic techniques to mediate the conflict. You could start by actively listening to both sides, saying, "I understand that Alex is concerned about the timeline, and Jamie wants to ensure we don't overlook any important details. How can we balance these priorities to move forward effectively?" By using neutral language, focusing on the issue, and encouraging collaboration, you help both parties see that their goals are not mutually exclusive and guide them toward a solution.

Real-World Examples of Successful Conflict Resolution

Example 1: Resolving a Client Dispute in a Marketing Agency

In a marketing agency, a conflict arose between the account manager and the creative team. The account manager wanted to meet the client's demands quickly, while the creative team felt the client's requests compromised the quality of the work. The account manager, not in a formal leadership role over the creative team, used diplomatic conflict resolution techniques to address the issue. They actively listened to the creative team's concerns, empathized with their desire to maintain high standards, and facilitated a meeting where both sides could express their views. By focusing on the shared goal of client satisfaction and using neutral language, the account manager helped the team reach a compromise that met the client's needs without sacrificing quality. This approach not only resolved the conflict but also strengthened the relationship between the account manager and the creative team.

Example 2: Managing Conflict in a Cross-Functional Project

In a cross-functional project team, conflict arose between the engineering and sales departments. The engineers were focused on creating a technically perfect product, while the sales team was concerned about time-to-market and customer demands. A project coordinator without formal authority over either department stepped in to mediate. They used empathy and active listening to understand each department's priorities and facilitated a discussion to find common ground. By reframing the conflict as a shared challenge—delivering a high-quality product on time—they helped the team align on a strategy that balanced technical excellence with market needs. This diplomatic approach led to a successful product launch and improved collaboration between the departments.

DRIVING CHANGE WITHOUT BEING IN CHARGE

In any organization, driving change can be challenging, especially when you don't have formal authority. However, it is entirely possible to influence change effectively by employing strategic approaches. As an organizational change consultant, I will outline strategies that can help you build coalitions, present compelling cases for change, and sustain momentum, even when you lack formal authority. These strategies, backed by real-world examples, will guide you through the process of influencing change in a professional and structured manner.

STRATEGIES FOR INFLUENCING ORGANIZATIONAL CHANGE

Before delving into specific strategies, it's essential to understand the context in which you are operating. Organizational change often involves shifting deeply ingrained behaviors, processes, and mindsets. As someone without formal authority, your ability to influence change will depend on your understanding of the organization's culture, the key stakeholders involved, and the potential barriers to change.

Building Coalitions for Change

One of the most effective ways to influence change without formal authority is by building coalitions. A coalition is a group of individuals who share a common goal and work together to achieve it. In the context of organizational change, coalitions can provide the support and collective power needed to drive change from within.

Identifying Potential Allies

The first step in building a coalition is to identify potential allies within the organization. These are individuals who share your vision for change or who stand to benefit from the proposed changes. Potential allies could include colleagues at the same level, influential team members, or even those in other departments who recognize the need for change.

Example: Building a Coalition for Process Improvement

Consider a scenario where you believe the organization's project management processes are inefficient and need to be streamlined. Without formal authority, you could start by identifying colleagues who are frustrated with the current processes and who would benefit from improvements. By discussing your ideas with them, you can begin to build a coalition of like-minded individuals who are willing to support the initiative.

Engaging Stakeholders

Once you have identified potential allies, the next step is to engage key stakeholders. Stakeholders are individuals or groups who have an interest in the outcome of the change initiative. They could be team members, managers, or even clients. Engaging stakeholders involves understanding their concerns, addressing their needs, and gaining their support for the change.

Example: Engaging Stakeholders in a Change Initiative

Suppose you are working in a marketing department and believe that adopting a new digital marketing strategy would benefit the organization. To engage stakeholders, you could present data on the benefits of digital marketing to your colleagues and managers, showing how it could increase the department's effectiveness. By addressing their concerns and demonstrating the value of the change, you can gain their support.

Leveraging Informal Networks

In many organizations, informal networks play a crucial role in influencing change. These networks are the relationships and connections that exist outside the formal hierarchy. By leveraging these networks, you can spread your ideas and gain support for change across different parts of the organization.

Example: Leveraging Informal Networks

Imagine you work in a large organization where communication between departments is limited. To drive change, you could leverage your informal network by reaching out to colleagues in other departments who are open to new ideas. By sharing your vision for change through these informal channels, you can build broader support and create momentum for the initiative.

Presenting a Compelling Case for Change

Even with a strong coalition, it's essential to present a compelling case for change to gain widespread support. A well-structured argument can persuade others to see the value in your proposed changes and commit to supporting them.

Developing a Clear Vision

A clear vision is the cornerstone of any successful change initiative. Your vision should articulate what the change will achieve and why it is necessary. It should be specific, realistic, and aligned with the organization's goals. A compelling vision can inspire others and provide a sense of direction for the change effort.

Example: Articulating a Vision for Change

If you are advocating for the adoption of a new technology platform, your vision might be: "By implementing this platform, we will streamline our operations, reduce manual errors, and enhance our ability to meet client needs, ultimately positioning our organization as a leader in the industry."

Using Data and Evidence

Supporting your case with data and evidence is crucial for convincing others of the need for change. Quantitative data, such as performance metrics, financial analyses, or customer feedback, can provide objective proof that change is necessary. Qualitative evidence, such as case studies or testimonials, can also be powerful in illustrating the benefits of the proposed changes.

Example: Using Data to Support a Change Initiative

Suppose you are advocating for a change in the organization's customer service approach. You could gather data on customer satisfaction scores, highlighting areas where the current approach is falling short. Additionally, you might present case studies from other organizations that have successfully implemented similar changes, demonstrating the potential benefits.

Tailoring the Message to Your Audience

Different stakeholders may have different concerns and priorities. Tailoring your message to address these specific needs can increase the likelihood of gaining their support. For example, senior management might be most concerned with the financial impact of the change, while frontline employees might be more interested in how the change will affect their day-to-day work.

Example: Tailoring the Message for Different Stakeholders

In advocating for a new employee training program, you might emphasize the program's potential to improve productivity and reduce costs when speaking to executives. Conversely, when discussing the same program with employees, you could focus on how it will enhance their skills and career development opportunities.

Sustaining Momentum for Change

Gaining initial support for change is only the beginning. Sustaining momentum over time is crucial to ensuring that the change is fully implemented and that it achieves the desired outcomes.

Creating Quick Wins

Quick wins are small, early successes that can demonstrate the value of the change initiative and build confidence among stakeholders. By achieving and publicizing these quick wins, you can generate positive momentum and encourage continued support for the change.

Example: Creating Quick Wins in a Change Initiative

If you are leading a change initiative to improve employee engagement, you might start by implementing a few small, visible changes, such as introducing regular team-building activities or enhancing internal communication channels. When employees see the immediate benefits of these changes, they are more likely to support the broader initiative.

Keeping Communication Open

Ongoing communication is essential for sustaining momentum. Regular updates, progress reports, and opportunities for feedback can keep stakeholders informed and engaged. Open communication also allows you to address any concerns or resistance that may arise as the change progresses.

Example: Maintaining Communication during a Change Initiative

During a company-wide initiative to implement a new software system, you could establish regular meetings or newsletters to update employees on the progress of the implementation, share success stories, and address any challenges. This keeps the momentum going and ensures that everyone remains committed to the change.

Addressing Resistance

Resistance is a natural part of any change process. Addressing resistance effectively involves understanding the underlying concerns and working to alleviate them. This might involve providing additional training, clarifying misunderstandings, or adjusting the change initiative to better meet the needs of those involved.

Example: Addressing Resistance to Change

Imagine that some employees are resistant to a proposed change in workflow because they fear it will increase their workload. To address this, you could offer additional training to help them adapt to the new workflow more efficiently, or you might work with them to find ways to streamline their existing tasks, so the overall impact on their workload is minimized.

Celebrating Successes

Celebrating successes, both big and small, can help maintain enthusiasm and commitment to the change initiative. Recognizing the efforts of those involved and highlighting the positive outcomes of the change can reinforce the value of the initiative and motivate others to continue supporting it.

Example: Celebrating Success in a Change Initiative

After successfully implementing a new performance management system, you might hold a celebration event to recognize the hard work of the team members involved. During the event, you could share positive feedback from employees and managers who have benefited from the new system, reinforcing the success of the initiative.

Real-World Examples of Influencing Change without Formal Authority

Example 1: Implementing a New Sustainability Initiative

In a mid-sized company, a group of employees without formal authority recognized the need for more sustainable business practices. They formed a coalition of like-minded colleagues from various departments and presented a compelling case to management, supported by data on the cost savings and environmental benefits of sustainability. They achieved quick wins by introducing small changes, such as reducing paper usage and improving recycling efforts. Over time, their initiative gained momentum, leading to the implementation of a company-wide sustainability program.

Example 2: Driving Cultural Change in a Sales Department

A sales representative in a large organization noticed that the department's culture was overly competitive, leading to high turnover and low morale. Without formal authority, she built a coalition of colleagues who shared her concerns and presented a case for change to the sales manager. By highlighting the long-term benefits of a more collaborative culture, including increased employee retention and improved team performance, she gained the manager's support. The team began implementing small changes, such as recognizing teamwork in performance evaluations, which gradually shifted the department's culture toward greater collaboration.

LEADING INNOVATION FROM ANY POSITION

Innovation is the lifeblood of any successful organization. It fuels growth, adapts to changing markets, and creates new opportunities. However, leading innovation is often thought of as the responsibility of those in formal leadership positions.

This assumption overlooks the powerful role that individuals without titles can play in driving innovation within their organizations. Whether you're a junior employee, a middle manager, or in any other non-leadership role, you have the potential to lead change, foster creativity, and influence the direction of your organization.

Fostering a Creative Environment

The first step in leading innovation is to create an environment where creativity can thrive. A creative environment encourages employees to think outside the box, experiment with new ideas, and take calculated risks. Even if you're not in a leadership role, you can contribute to this environment by modeling creative behavior, encouraging others to share their ideas, and providing constructive feedback.

Encouraging Open Communication

Open communication is essential for fostering creativity. When employees feel safe to express their thoughts and ideas without fear of judgment, they are more likely to contribute innovative solutions. As someone without formal authority, you can encourage open communication by actively listening to your colleagues, asking thought-provoking questions, and validating their contributions.

Example: Creating a Culture of Open Communication

Consider the case of a mid-level software engineer named Sarah who worked in a tech company. Sarah noticed that her team was hesitant to share ideas during meetings, leading to a stagnant flow of innovation. Without a formal leadership title, she began to initiate informal brainstorming sessions where team members could freely share ideas. She made it clear that all ideas were welcome and that the purpose was to explore possibilities without immediate judgment. Over time, these sessions became a regular practice, and the team started to generate more creative solutions. Sarah's efforts helped foster a culture of open communication, leading to several successful product innovations.

Promoting Psychological Safety

Psychological safety is the belief that one can speak up, take risks, and make mistakes without facing negative consequences. In a psychologically safe environment, employees are more likely to engage in innovative behavior. You can promote psychological safety by being supportive of others' ideas, acknowledging your own mistakes, and fostering an atmosphere of mutual respect.

John, a marketing coordinator in a large corporation, observed that his colleagues were reluctant to propose new marketing strategies because they feared criticism from upper management. Although John did not have formal authority, he started to openly discuss his own mistakes and what he learned from them during team meetings. This transparency encouraged others to do the same, and gradually, the team became more comfortable experimenting with new ideas. John's efforts led to the successful implementation of several innovative marketing campaigns.

Championing New Ideas

Innovation requires not only the generation of new ideas but also the ability to champion them within the organization. As a non-title leader, your role in championing innovation involves advocating for ideas, building support, and guiding them through the implementation process.

Building a Business Case

To gain support for a new idea, it's important to build a compelling business case that outlines the benefits, potential risks, and feasibility of the idea. Even if you don't have the authority to make final decisions, presenting a well-thought-out business case can influence those who do.

Example: Building a Business Case

Alex, a junior analyst at a financial services firm, identified an opportunity to improve the firm's data analysis processes using a new software tool. Although he lacked the authority to implement the tool, Alex conducted thorough research, including cost-benefit analysis, potential ROI, and case studies from other companies that had successfully used the software. He presented his findings to his manager, who was impressed by the thoroughness of the proposal. The idea was eventually approved, leading to significant efficiency gains for the firm.

Gathering Allies and Building Coalitions

Securing buy-in from stakeholders often requires building a coalition of supporters who can advocate for the idea alongside you. This coalition can include colleagues, managers, and even external partners who see the value in the proposed innovation.

Example: Building a Coalition for Innovation

Consider the case of Maria, a project manager in a manufacturing company. She identified a new technology that could significantly reduce production costs, but she knew that convincing the leadership team would be challenging. Maria began by discussing the idea with her colleagues in the engineering and finance departments, both of whom would be directly impacted by the change. By gathering data and aligning her proposal with the company's strategic goals, Maria was able to build a strong coalition of supporters. Together, they presented the idea to senior management, who approved the implementation of the new technology, resulting in substantial cost savings.

Navigating Organizational Politics

Navigating organizational politics is a critical skill for championing new ideas, especially when you don't hold formal authority. Understanding the power dynamics, knowing who the key decision-makers are, and aligning your proposal with the organization's strategic priorities can significantly increase your chances of success.

Example: Navigating Organizational Politics

Daniel, a product designer at a consumer electronics company, had an idea for a new feature that he believed would be a game-changer for the company's flagship product. However, he knew that the senior leadership team was focused on cost reduction and might be hesitant to invest in new features. To navigate this challenge, Daniel aligned his proposal with the company's cost-saving goals by demonstrating how the new feature could increase product sales and customer retention, ultimately offsetting the initial investment. By framing his idea within the context of the company's priorities, Daniel successfully secured approval for the feature, which became a key selling point for the product.

Securing Buy-In from Stakeholders

Securing buy-in from stakeholders is crucial for turning innovative ideas into reality. Without the formal authority to mandate changes, you must rely on your ability to persuade and influence others.

Communicating the Value of Innovation

To secure buy-in, it's essential to clearly communicate the value of the proposed innovation. This includes explaining how the idea aligns with the organization's goals, addressing potential concerns, and highlighting the benefits for both the organization and the individuals involved.

Example: Communicating the Value of Innovation

Linda, an operations coordinator in a logistics company, proposed a new routing software that could optimize delivery routes and reduce fuel costs. However, the implementation required a significant upfront investment, and some team members were skeptical. Linda communicated the value of the innovation by providing data on potential cost savings, environmental benefits, and improved customer satisfaction. She also addressed concerns about the transition process by proposing a phased implementation plan. Her clear communication and thorough preparation helped secure buy-in from both her team and upper management.

Engaging Influential Stakeholders

Influential stakeholders, such as department heads or key decision-makers, can significantly impact the success of your innovation efforts. Engaging these individuals early in the process and addressing their specific concerns can help you gain their support.

Example: Engaging Influential Stakeholders

Raj, a mid-level IT specialist, developed a proposal for a cloud-based system that could improve the company's data security and reduce maintenance costs. Recognizing the importance of senior leadership support, Raj scheduled meetings with key stakeholders, including the CFO and the head of IT, to discuss his proposal. He tailored his presentation to address their concerns about cost, security, and scalability. By engaging these influential stakeholders and aligning his proposal with their priorities, Raj successfully gained the support needed to implement the new system.

Sustaining Innovation Momentum

Innovation is not a one-time event but an ongoing process. Sustaining momentum requires continuous effort, adaptability, and a commitment to fostering a culture of innovation within the organization.

Creating a Culture of Continuous Improvement

A culture of continuous improvement encourages employees to consistently seek ways to innovate and improve processes. As a non-title leader, you can contribute to this culture by promoting the idea that innovation is everyone's responsibility and by celebrating small wins along the way.

Example: Creating a Culture of Continuous Improvement

Megan, a customer service representative at a retail company, noticed that her team often struggled with outdated procedures that frustrated both employees and customers. Without formal authority, Megan started a "Process Improvement Club," where team members could come together to discuss challenges and propose solutions. The club's informal nature encouraged participation, and the team began implementing small changes that gradually improved efficiency and customer satisfaction. Megan's initiative not only led to process improvements but also fostered a culture of continuous innovation within the team.

Recognizing and Rewarding Innovation

Recognizing and rewarding innovation can motivate employees to continue contributing new ideas. While you may not have the authority to offer formal rewards, you can acknowledge the efforts of your colleagues through verbal recognition, public praise, or by advocating for their ideas to be implemented.

Example: Recognizing Innovation in a Team Setting

In a marketing agency, a junior graphic designer named Ethan came up with a unique branding concept that resonated well with a key client. Although he wasn't in a leadership position, Ethan's idea was a hit, and the client decided to adopt the new branding. The team leader publicly recognized Ethan's contribution during a team meeting and advocated for him to present his concept to the client. This recognition not only boosted Ethan's confidence but also encouraged others in the team to share their creative ideas.

Real-World Case Studies of Innovation from Non-Leadership Roles

Case Study 1: The Development of Gmail by Paul Buchheit

Paul Buchheit was a software engineer at Google who, without holding a senior leadership position, spearheaded the development of Gmail. He saw the potential for a better email system that could handle large amounts of storage and allow for efficient searching of emails. Buchheit worked on the project during his "20% time"—a Google policy that allowed employees to spend 20% of their time on side projects. Despite initial skepticism from some leaders, Buchheit persisted, building a prototype and gaining support from other engineers and eventually from Google's founders. Gmail's success revolutionized email services and demonstrated the power of innovation from non-leadership roles.

Case Study 2 Leading Innovation Without a Title: Strategies for Driving Creativity and Change**

Innovation is essential for any organization's growth and adaptability, but leading innovation is often mistakenly seen as the responsibility of those in formal leadership positions. However, individuals without titles can play a crucial role in driving creativity and influencing change within their organizations. This section will explore strategies for fostering a creative environment, championing new ideas, securing buy-in from stakeholders, and sustaining innovation momentum, regardless of your formal title. Real-world examples will illustrate how these strategies can be successfully implemented in any organizational setting.

Fostering a Creative Environment

Creating an environment where creativity can flourish is the first step in leading innovation. A creative environment encourages experimentation, embraces failure as a learning opportunity, and supports diverse perspectives. Even without formal authority, you can contribute to fostering such an environment by modeling creative behavior, encouraging others to share their ideas, and providing constructive feedback.

Encouraging Open Communication

Open communication is vital for creativity. When team members feel safe expressing their thoughts and ideas without fear of judgment, they are more likely to contribute innovative solutions. As someone without formal authority, you can foster open communication by actively listening to your colleagues, asking thought-provoking questions, and validating their contributions.

Example: Creating a Culture of Open Communication

Sarah, a mid-level software engineer at a tech company, noticed that her team was hesitant to share ideas during meetings, leading to stagnation. To address this, she initiated informal brainstorming sessions where team members could freely share ideas. Over time, these sessions became a regular practice, and the team started to generate more creative solutions, leading to several successful product innovations.

Promoting Psychological Safety

Psychological safety—the belief that one can speak up, take risks, and make mistakes without facing negative consequences—is crucial for innovation. You can promote psychological safety by being supportive of others' ideas, acknowledging your own mistakes, and fostering an atmosphere of mutual respect.

Example: Promoting Psychological Safety

John, a marketing coordinator in a large corporation, noticed that his colleagues were reluctant to propose new marketing strategies due to fear of criticism from upper management. John began openly discussing his own mistakes and what he learned from them during team meetings. This transparency encouraged others to do the same, and gradually, the team became more comfortable experimenting with new ideas.

John's efforts led to the successful implementation of several innovative marketing campaigns.

Championing New Ideas

Innovation requires not only generating new ideas but also championing them within the organization. As a non-title leader, you can play a crucial role in advocating for ideas, building support, and guiding them through the implementation process.

Building a Business Case

To gain support for a new idea, it's essential to build a compelling business case that outlines the benefits, potential risks, and feasibility of the idea. Even without the authority to make final decisions, presenting a well-thought-out business case can influence those who do.

Example: Building a Business Case

Alex, a junior analyst at a financial services firm, identified an opportunity to improve the firm's data analysis processes using a new software tool. Although he lacked the authority to implement the tool, Alex conducted thorough research, including cost-benefit analysis, potential ROI, and case studies from other companies that had successfully used the software.

He presented his findings to his manager, who was impressed by the thoroughness of the proposal. The idea was eventually approved, leading to significant efficiency gains for the firm.

Gathering Allies and Building Coalitions

Securing buy-in from stakeholders often requires building a coalition of supporters who can advocate for the idea alongside you. This coalition can include colleagues, managers, and even external partners who see the value in the proposed innovation.

Example: Building a Coalition for Innovation

Maria, a project manager in a manufacturing company, identified a new technology that could significantly reduce production costs, but she knew that convincing the leadership team would be challenging. Maria began by discussing the idea with her colleagues in the engineering and finance departments, both of whom would be directly impacted by the change. By gathering data and aligning her proposal with the company's strategic goals, Maria was able to build a strong coalition of supporters. Together, they presented the idea to senior management, who approved the implementation of the new technology, resulting in substantial cost savings.

Navigating Organizational Politics

Navigating organizational politics is a critical skill for championing new ideas, especially when you don't hold formal authority. Understanding the power dynamics, knowing who the key decision-makers are, and aligning your proposal with the organization's strategic priorities can significantly increase your chances of success.

Example: Navigating Organizational Politics

Daniel, a product designer at a consumer electronics company, had an idea for a new feature that he believed would be a game-changer for the company's flagship product. However, he knew that the senior leadership team was focused on cost reduction and might be hesitant to invest in new features. To navigate this challenge, Daniel aligned his proposal with the company's cost-saving goals by demonstrating how the new feature could increase product sales and customer retention, ultimately offsetting the initial investment. By framing his idea within the context of the company's priorities, Daniel successfully secured approval for the feature, which became a key selling point for the product.

Securing Buy-In from Stakeholders

Securing buy-in from stakeholders is crucial for turning innovative ideas into reality. Without the formal authority to mandate changes, you must rely on your ability to persuade and influence others.

Communicating the Value of Innovation

To secure buy-in, it's essential to clearly communicate the value of the proposed innovation. This includes explaining how the idea aligns with the organization's goals, addressing potential concerns, and highlighting the benefits for both the organization and the individuals involved.

Example: Communicating the Value of Innovation

Linda, an operations coordinator in a logistics company, proposed a new routing software that could optimize delivery routes and reduce fuel costs. However, the implementation required a significant upfront investment, and some team members were skeptical. Linda communicated the value of the innovation by providing data on potential cost savings, environmental benefits, and improved customer satisfaction. She also addressed concerns about the transition process by proposing a phased implementation plan. Her clear communication and thorough preparation helped secure buy-in from both her team and upper management.

Engaging Influential Stakeholders

Influential stakeholders, such as department heads or key decision-makers, can significantly impact the success of your innovation efforts. Engaging these individuals early in the process and addressing their specific concerns can help you gain their support.

Example: Engaging Influential Stakeholders

Raj, a mid-level IT specialist, developed a proposal for a cloud-based system that could improve the company's data security and reduce maintenance costs. Recognizing the importance of senior leadership support, Raj scheduled meetings with key stakeholders, including the CFO and the head of IT, to discuss his proposal. He tailored his presentation to address their concerns about cost, security, and scalability. By engaging these influential stakeholders and aligning his proposal with their priorities, Raj successfully gained the support needed to implement the new system.

Sustaining Innovation Momentum

Innovation is not a one-time event but an ongoing process. Sustaining momentum requires continuous effort, adaptability, and a commitment to fostering a culture of innovation within the organization.

Creating a Culture of Continuous Improvement

A culture of continuous improvement encourages employees to consistently seek ways to innovate and improve processes. As a non-title leader, you can contribute to this culture by promoting the idea that innovation is everyone's responsibility and by celebrating small wins along the way.

Example: Creating a Culture of Continuous Improvement

Megan, a customer service representative at a retail company, noticed that her team often struggled with outdated procedures that frustrated both employees and customers. Without formal authority, Megan started a "Process Improvement Club," where team members could come together to discuss challenges and propose solutions. The club's informal nature encouraged participation, and the team began implementing small changes that gradually improved efficiency and customer satisfaction. Megan's initiative not only led to process improvements but also fostered a culture of continuous innovation within the team.

Recognizing and Rewarding Innovation

Recognizing and rewarding innovation can motivate employees to continue contributing new ideas. While you may not have the authority to offer formal rewards, you can acknowledge the efforts of your colleagues through verbal recognition, public praise, or by advocating for their ideas to be implemented.

Example: Recognizing Innovation in a Team Setting

In a marketing agency, a junior graphic designer named Ethan came up with a unique branding concept that resonated well with a key client. Although he wasn't in a leadership position, Ethan's idea was a hit, and the client decided to adopt the new branding. The team leader publicly recognized Ethan's contribution during a team meeting and advocated for him to present his concept to the client. This recognition not only boosted Ethan's confidence but also encouraged others in the team to share their creative ideas.

PART IV: NAVIGATING ORGANIZATIONAL CHALLENGES

MANAGING UP: INFLUENCING YOUR SUPERIORS

Upward communication, the process of conveying information from subordinates to superiors, is critical in any organization. It fosters transparency, promotes collaboration, and enables employees to contribute to decision-making processes. As a communication expert, this guide will provide strategies for effective upward communication, focusing on how to present ideas to superiors, manage expectations, and build a strong rapport with leadership. The aim is to equip you with practical tools to enhance your communication effectiveness and ensure your voice is heard in the higher echelons of your organization.

EFFECTIVE UPWARD COMMUNICATION TECHNIQUES

Upward communication serves as the backbone of organizational transparency and collaboration. It allows leaders to gain insights from their team members, fostering a culture of inclusivity and shared responsibility. Effective upward communication helps bridge the gap between different levels of an organization, ensuring that valuable ideas and feedback flow seamlessly from employees to management. When done correctly, it can lead to improved decision-making, increased employee engagement, and overall organizational success.

Building a Foundation: Understanding Your Audience

Before you can effectively communicate upward, it's essential to understand the audience you're addressing—your superiors. Knowing their communication style, preferences, and expectations will enable you to tailor your approach accordingly.

1. Research and Understand Leadership Styles

Take the time to observe and understand the communication styles of your superiors. Are they detail-oriented, or do they prefer high-level summaries? Do they value data-driven insights, or are they more interested in creative ideas? Tailoring your communication to their preferences will increase the likelihood of your message being received positively.

2. Align Your Message with Organizational Goals

Frame your ideas in a way that aligns with the organization's objectives. When presenting ideas, emphasize how they contribute to achieving the company's strategic goals. This approach not only demonstrates your understanding of the bigger picture but also shows that you are invested in the organization's success.

Presenting Ideas Effectively

When presenting ideas to superiors, clarity, and conciseness are paramount. Your goal is to convey your message in a way that is easy to understand and compelling enough to warrant action.

1. Start with a Strong Opening

Begin your communication with a clear and compelling opening statement. This could be a summary of the issue you're addressing, the solution you're proposing, or the benefits of your idea. A strong opening sets the tone for the rest of the conversation and captures your superior's attention.

2. Use Data and Evidence to Support Your Ideas

Back up your proposals with data, research, and evidence. Presenting well-researched information not only strengthens your argument but also demonstrates your commitment to making informed decisions. For instance, if you're proposing a new project, include metrics or case studies that highlight the potential benefits.

3. Be Clear and Concise

Avoid overwhelming your audience with too much information. Focus on the key points that support your idea and deliver them in a clear and concise manner. Use bullet points or numbered lists to break down complex information, making it easier for your superior to follow.

4. Anticipate Questions and Concerns

Think ahead about the potential questions or concerns your superiors might have regarding your proposal. Address these proactively in your presentation, showing that you have considered all aspects of the idea. This approach not only demonstrates thoroughness but also builds confidence in your proposal.

5. Offer Solutions, Not Just Problems

When raising issues or challenges, always accompany them with potential solutions. This proactive approach shows that you are not just identifying problems but are also invested in finding ways to resolve them.

Managing Expectations

Effective upward communication is not just about presenting ideas but also about managing expectations. This involves setting realistic goals, being transparent about potential challenges, and ensuring that your superiors are fully aware of what can be achieved.

1. Set Clear and Realistic Expectations

When proposing ideas or projects, be honest about the potential outcomes and limitations. Setting realistic expectations helps build trust and ensures that there are no surprises later on. For example, if you're proposing a new initiative, outline the expected timeline, resources required, and any potential risks.

2. Communicate Progress Regularly

Once your idea is approved, maintain regular communication with your superiors about the progress. Provide updates on key milestones, challenges encountered, and any adjustments needed. This ongoing communication helps manage expectations and keeps your superiors informed and engaged in the process.

3. Be Transparent About Challenges

If you encounter obstacles or delays, communicate them promptly. Transparency is key to maintaining trust and ensuring that your superiors are aware of the situation. When discussing challenges, always accompany them with potential solutions or a revised plan to demonstrate that you are still in control of the situation.

4. Seek Feedback and Be Open to Criticism

Encourage feedback from your superiors and be open to constructive criticism. This not only shows that you are willing to learn and improve but also helps refine your ideas and approach. Incorporating feedback into your work demonstrates adaptability and a commitment to continuous improvement.

BUILDING A STRONG RAPPORT WITH LEADERSHIP

Building a strong rapport with your superiors is essential for effective upward communication. A positive relationship with leadership can facilitate open dialogue, increase trust, and make it easier to gain support for your ideas.

1. Demonstrate Reliability and Integrity

Consistently delivering on your promises and maintaining high ethical standards will earn you the trust and respect of your superiors. When they see that you are reliable and have integrity, they are more likely to take your ideas and feedback seriously.

2. Show Initiative and Proactivity

Take the initiative to address issues or propose improvements without waiting to be asked. Proactivity demonstrates your commitment to the organization and your willingness to go above and beyond your regular duties. For example, if you notice a process that could be improved, take the lead in researching solutions and presenting them to your superior.

3. Engage in Regular, Informal Communication

Building rapport goes beyond formal meetings and presentations. Engage in regular, informal communication with your superiors. This could be through casual conversations, emails, or brief updates on ongoing projects. Regular interaction helps build familiarity and trust, making it easier to communicate when it matters most.

4. Understand and Support Leadership's Priorities

Take the time to understand your superior's priorities and challenges. Show support by aligning your work with their goals and offering assistance when possible. Demonstrating that you are invested in their success as well as your own will strengthen your relationship.

5. Show Appreciation and Acknowledge Support

When your superiors support your ideas or provide guidance, be sure to express your appreciation. Acknowledging their support fosters goodwill and encourages continued collaboration. Whether it's a simple thank-you email or public recognition during a meeting, showing gratitude goes a long way in building a positive relationship.

Examples of Successful Upward Communication

1. The Case of Jane, the Operations Coordinator

Jane, an operations coordinator in a manufacturing company, identified a bottleneck in the production process that was causing delays and increased costs. She conducted a thorough analysis and proposed a new workflow that would streamline operations. Jane presented her findings to her manager, using data and a clear cost-benefit analysis to support her proposal. Her manager was impressed with the thoroughness of her work and approved the new process, which led to a significant increase in efficiency and cost savings.

2. The Story of Mike, the Marketing Analyst

Mike, a marketing analyst at a mid-sized firm, noticed that the company's social media strategy was outdated and not yielding the desired results. He took the initiative to research current trends and developed a comprehensive strategy that included targeted advertising and content marketing. Mike presented his proposal to the head of marketing, emphasizing the potential for increased engagement and revenue. His well-prepared presentation and data-driven approach convinced the leadership to adopt the new strategy, which resulted in a significant boost in the company's online presence and sales.

Building Strong Relationships with Leaders

Building strong, trust-based relationships with organizational leaders is a crucial aspect of professional success. These relationships not only help you align more effectively with the goals of your organization but also pave the way for career advancement. As a leadership advisor, this guide will provide strategies for aligning with leadership goals, demonstrating value, and maintaining transparency. Real-world examples will illustrate how cultivating strong relationships with leaders can lead to significant career growth.

Understanding the Importance of Trust in Leadership Relationships

Trust is the foundation of any strong relationship, particularly in a professional setting. When trust exists between employees and leaders, it fosters open communication, collaboration, and a shared commitment to organizational goals. Trust-based relationships enable you to work more closely with leaders, understand their vision, and contribute meaningfully to the organization's success.

Building trust with leaders requires consistent effort and a deep understanding of their goals, challenges, and expectations. Trust is earned over time through actions that demonstrate reliability, competence, and integrity.

Aligning with Leadership Goals

One of the most effective ways to build strong relationships with organizational leaders is to align your efforts with their goals. Leaders are more likely to trust and value employees who understand and support their vision for the organization.

1. Understand the Leadership Vision

Start by gaining a clear understanding of the leadership's vision and strategic objectives. This may involve attending meetings, reading company reports, or having direct conversations with leaders. Understanding their goals allows you to tailor your work to support their priorities.

2. Proactively Offer Solutions

Once you understand the leadership's goals, look for ways to contribute to them. This might involve proposing new ideas, streamlining processes, or identifying areas where you can add value. Leaders appreciate employees who take the initiative to solve problems and contribute to the organization's success.

3. Align Your Goals with Organizational Objectives

Ensure that your personal and professional goals align with the broader objectives of the organization. This alignment not only helps you stay focused on the right tasks but also demonstrates your commitment to the organization's success.

4. Communicate Your Alignment

Regularly communicate with your leaders about how your work aligns with their goals. This can be done through status updates, meetings, or informal conversations. By keeping leaders informed, you reinforce your commitment to their vision and build trust over time.

Demonstrating Value to Leadership

Demonstrating your value to leadership involves consistently delivering results, showcasing your expertise, and contributing to the organization's success. When leaders see the tangible impact of your work, they are more likely to trust and rely on you.

1. Deliver Consistent Results

Reliability is key to building trust with leaders. Consistently delivering high-quality work on time shows that you are dependable and can be trusted to meet your commitments. Leaders need to know that they can count on you to achieve the results they expect.

2. Showcase Your Expertise

Position yourself as an expert in your field by sharing your knowledge and insights with leaders. This could involve presenting data-driven reports, offering advice on specific issues, or leading initiatives in your area of expertise. Demonstrating your knowledge and skills helps establish your credibility and value to the organization.

3. Go beyond Your Job Description

Don't limit yourself to the tasks outlined in your job description. Look for opportunities to take on additional responsibilities, lead projects, or mentor colleagues. Going above and beyond shows that you are invested in the organization's success and are willing to contribute in any way you can.

4. Be a Problem Solver

Leaders value employees who can identify and solve problems without needing constant supervision. Whether it's improving a process, resolving conflicts, or finding new efficiencies, being proactive in addressing challenges demonstrates your value and builds trust with leadership.

Maintaining Transparency

Transparency is essential in building and maintaining trust-based relationships with organizational leaders. Being open and honest in your communications, acknowledging your limitations, and keeping leaders informed about your progress are all key components of transparency.

1. Communicate Openly and Honestly

Always be transparent in your communications with leaders. If you encounter challenges or make mistakes, address them openly rather than trying to cover them up. Honesty builds trust, while dishonesty can quickly erode it.

2. Acknowledge Your Limitations

No one expects you to have all the answers. Acknowledging your limitations and seeking help when needed shows humility and a willingness to learn. Leaders respect employees who are honest about their capabilities and are committed to personal growth.

3. Provide Regular Updates

Keep leaders informed about your progress on key projects and initiatives. Regular updates help maintain transparency and ensure that leaders are aware of any developments that may impact their goals. This also allows for early intervention if any issues arise, preventing small problems from becoming major obstacles.

4. Be Accountable

Take responsibility for your actions, both successes and failures. Accountability is a cornerstone of trust and demonstrates your commitment to the organization's success. When leaders see that you are accountable, they are more likely to trust you with greater responsibilities.

Real-World Examples of Strong Leadership Relationships

Example 1: The Case of Sarah, the Marketing Manager

Sarah was a marketing manager at a tech startup. From the beginning, she made an effort to understand the CEO's vision of expanding the company's market presence. Sarah aligned her marketing strategies with this vision and consistently communicated her progress to the CEO. She also took the initiative to lead a new product launch, which was a major success. Her efforts didn't go unnoticed; the CEO began to rely on Sarah for advice on other strategic decisions. Eventually, Sarah was promoted to Vice President of Marketing, a role in which she continues to drive the company's growth.

Example 2: The Story of James, the Operations Analyst

James worked as an operations analyst at a manufacturing company. He noticed inefficiencies in the production process that were affecting the company's bottom line. James conducted a thorough analysis and proposed a solution to the COO. He communicated his findings clearly, backed up by data, and demonstrated how his solution aligned with the company's cost-saving goals. The COO was impressed with James's initiative and transparency, leading to the implementation of the new process. As a result, the company saw significant cost reductions, and James was soon promoted to a management position, where he continues to contribute to the company's operational efficiency.

The Impact of Strong Relationships with Leaders

Building strong, trust-based relationships with organizational leaders can have a profound impact on your career. These relationships not only provide opportunities for career advancement but also enhance your ability to influence decision-making and drive organizational success.

1. Career Advancement

Strong relationships with leaders often lead to career growth and advancement. When leaders trust you and value your contributions, they are more likely to consider you for promotions, leadership roles, and other opportunities. As seen in the examples of Sarah and James, building trust with leaders can accelerate your career trajectory.

2. Increased Influence

Trust-based relationships with leaders give you greater influence within the organization. When leaders trust your judgment and expertise, they are more likely to seek your input on important decisions. This increased influence allows you to contribute more meaningfully to the organization's success.

3. Enhanced Job Satisfaction

Working in an environment where you have strong, positive relationships with leaders can lead to greater job satisfaction. When you feel trusted and valued, you are more motivated to perform at your best and contribute to the organization's goals.

This sense of fulfillment can have a positive impact on your overall well-being and career satisfaction.

4. Professional Growth

Building relationships with leaders also provides opportunities for professional growth and development. Through these relationships, you can gain valuable insights, mentorship, and feedback that help you grow as a professional. Leaders who trust and value you are more likely to invest in your development, providing you with the resources and support you need to succeed.

Conclusion

Building strong, trust-based relationships with organizational leaders is essential for career success. By aligning with leadership goals, demonstrating your value, and maintaining transparency, you can earn the trust and respect of your leaders. These relationships not only open doors for career advancement but also enhance your ability to influence decision-making and contribute to the organization's success. The examples provided illustrate how trust-based relationships with leaders can lead to significant career growth and professional fulfillment. As you continue to build and nurture these relationships, you will find yourself in a stronger position to achieve your career goals and make a meaningful impact within your organization.

OVERCOMING COMMON CHALLENGES OF NON-TITLE LEADERSHIP

Leading without a formal title can be both challenging and rewarding. One of the most significant hurdles is handling resistance and pushback from colleagues or team members who may not recognize your authority. As a leadership consultant, I will explore various strategies for addressing concerns, building alliances, and maintaining persistence, all of which are crucial for overcoming these challenges. Real-life examples will be included to illustrate how these strategies can be successfully implemented in a professional setting.

HANDLING RESISTANCE AND PUSHBACK

Resistance and pushback often stem from uncertainty, fear of change, or a perceived threat to the status quo. When leading without a formal title, it's essential to understand these underlying causes to address them effectively. Resistance may manifest as passive-aggressive behavior, outright refusal to cooperate, or subtle undermining of your efforts. Recognizing these signs early on is crucial for developing an appropriate response strategy.

Addressing Concerns with Empathy and Transparency

One of the first steps in handling resistance is addressing the concerns of those who are pushing back. This requires empathy, transparency, and open communication.

1. Listen Actively

Begin by listening to the concerns of those resisting your leadership. This shows that you value their opinions and are willing to understand their perspective. Active listening involves not just hearing the words but also paying attention to the emotions and motivations behind them. For instance, if a team member expresses concern about a new process, listen carefully to their fears and acknowledge them before offering your perspective.

2. Communicate Transparently

Transparency is key to building trust and alleviating concerns. Clearly explain your intentions, the reasons behind the changes or initiatives you're advocating for, and how they align with the organization's goals. By being open about your plans and the potential impact, you can reduce uncertainty and build support.

3. Address Fears Directly

Often, resistance is driven by fear—fear of failure, fear of the unknown, or fear of losing status or control. Address these fears directly by providing reassurances, offering support, and showing how the proposed changes can lead to positive outcomes for everyone involved.

Example: Overcoming Fear of Change

Consider the case of John, a project manager who had to lead a new digital transformation initiative without a formal leadership title. Some team members were resistant due to concerns about job security and the potential complexity of new technologies. John addressed these fears by organizing workshops to upskill the team, clearly communicating how the changes would enhance their roles rather than replace them, and being transparent about the timeline and goals. His approach helped to ease concerns and build a collaborative spirit among the team.

Building Alliances to Strengthen Your Position

Building alliances within the organization is crucial when leading without formal authority. Allies can help amplify your message, provide support, and lend credibility to your efforts.

1. Identify Key Stakeholders

Identify individuals within the organization who share your vision or who may benefit from the changes you are advocating. These could be peers, managers, or even subordinates who are influential within their own networks. Building relationships with these stakeholders can help you gain their support and influence others.

2. Leverage Informal Networks

Informal networks within an organization often wield significant influence. By tapping into these networks, you can gather support from a broader base, making it easier to overcome resistance. Engage with these networks through informal meetings, social events, or collaborative projects to build trust and rapport.

3. Create a Coalition of Supporters

A coalition of supporters can be powerful in driving change, especially when you lack formal authority. This group can help advocate for your ideas, provide diverse perspectives, and offer collective problem-solving capabilities. Encourage your allies to take ownership of certain aspects of the project, making them feel invested in the outcome.

Example: Building a Coalition for Change

Sarah, a mid-level employee at a healthcare organization, recognized the need for a new patient management system. Without formal authority, she began by gathering support from nurses and administrative staff who would benefit directly from the new system. She then reached out to IT staff to ensure technical feasibility and involved a few doctors to provide input on clinical integration. By building a coalition of diverse stakeholders, Sarah was able to gain the support needed to present a strong case to senior management, ultimately leading to the successful implementation of the system.

Maintaining Persistence in the Face of Pushback

Persistence is essential when leading without a title. Pushback is inevitable, but how you respond to it will determine your success.

1. Stay Committed to Your Vision

Persistence starts with a clear commitment to your vision. Stay focused on your goals, and don't be discouraged by initial resistance. Remind yourself and your team of the long-term benefits of the changes you are advocating for, and keep pushing forward, even when progress seems slow.

2. Adapt and Be Flexible

While persistence is important, it's also crucial to be adaptable. If a particular approach isn't working, be willing to adjust your strategy. Flexibility shows that you are responsive to feedback and willing to find the best possible solution, rather than rigidly sticking to a plan that isn't effective.

3. Celebrate Small Wins

Acknowledge and celebrate small victories along the way. These wins, no matter how minor, help maintain momentum and keep your team motivated. They also demonstrate progress to those who may still be skeptical, gradually reducing resistance.

Example: Persistence Leading to Success

Mark, a team leader in a manufacturing company, faced significant resistance when proposing a shift to a lean manufacturing approach. The pushback was strong, with concerns about increased workload and the viability of the new processes. Mark remained persistent, starting with a pilot program in one department to demonstrate the benefits. As the pilot showed positive results, he gradually expanded the approach, celebrating each milestone. His persistence paid off, and the lean manufacturing approach was eventually adopted company-wide, leading to improved efficiency and reduced costs.

Techniques for Addressing Concerns and Reducing Resistance

To effectively handle resistance, it's important to address concerns head-on and reduce the factors contributing to pushback.

1. Engage in Open Dialogue

Encourage open dialogue where team members can express their concerns and provide feedback. This creates a space for constructive criticism and allows you to address issues before they escalate into full-blown resistance.

2. Provide Support and Resources

Offer support and resources to help team members adjust to changes. This could include training, additional manpower, or even moral support. When people feel supported, they are more likely to embrace change rather than resist it.

3. Involve Resisters in the Process

Involve those who are resistant in the planning and implementation process. By giving them a role in shaping the changes, you reduce their sense of alienation and make them feel more invested in the outcome.

4. Clarify the Benefits

Clearly articulate the benefits of the proposed changes, both for the organization and for the individuals involved. When people see what's in it for them, they are more likely to support the initiative.

Example: Reducing Resistance through Inclusion

Emily, a software developer, faced resistance when suggesting a new coding framework to her team. The pushback came from senior developers who were comfortable with the existing system. Instead of imposing the new framework, Emily engaged these developers in discussions about the potential benefits, invited them to test the framework themselves, and incorporated their feedback into the final proposal. This inclusive approach reduced resistance and led to a smoother transition to the new framework.

Real-Life Examples of Overcoming Resistance

1. The Case of a Nonprofit Initiative

At a nonprofit organization, a junior program officer named Lisa identified the need for a new approach to donor engagement. However, she faced resistance from senior colleagues who were accustomed to traditional methods. Lisa addressed their concerns by presenting data on how other organizations had successfully implemented similar strategies. She also built alliances with younger staff who were more open to change and gradually gained the support of key decision-makers. Her persistence and strategic approach led to the adoption of the new donor engagement strategy, which resulted in increased donations and better donor relationships.

2. Transforming a Sales Team's Approach

In a sales team at a mid-sized company, a sales representative named Tom proposed a shift from cold calling to a more targeted, relationship-based approach. The idea faced significant pushback from colleagues who were used to the old methods. Tom addressed their concerns by providing training on the new approach, showing how it could lead to higher conversion rates, and involving key resisters in the development of the new strategy. Over time, as the team saw positive results from the new approach, resistance faded, and the entire sales team adopted the new method.

BALANCING AUTHORITY AND COLLABORATION

Balancing the need for authority with the importance of collaboration in leadership is a critical skill for organizational success. Effective leaders understand that while authority is necessary for making decisions and guiding a team, collaboration fosters creativity, innovation, and a sense of ownership among team members. This balance ensures that the leader can assert influence while also encouraging input and participation from others, creating a more dynamic and effective team environment.

The Role of Authority in Leadership

Authority in leadership is essential for setting direction, making decisions, and ensuring that the organization meets its goals. Leaders with authority have the power to allocate resources, assign tasks, and hold individuals accountable for their performance. However, relying solely on authority can lead to a top-down management style that stifles creativity, discourages initiative, and creates a disconnect between the leader and the team.

1. Establishing Clear Expectations

One of the primary functions of authority is to establish clear expectations. Leaders must set the tone for the organization by defining goals, roles, and responsibilities. This clarity helps team members understand what is expected of them and how their work contributes to the larger objectives of the organization. For example, a project manager might use their authority to define the scope of a project, assign tasks to team members, and set deadlines for deliverables.

2. Decision-Making Authority

Authority is also crucial in decision-making. Leaders are often required to make tough decisions that affect the entire organization. These decisions might involve resource allocation, strategic direction, or personnel changes. For instance, a CEO might decide to enter a new market, requiring the reallocation of resources and a shift in organizational focus. This decision, made through the exercise of authority, can have a significant impact on the organization's success.

3. Accountability and Performance Management

Authority enables leaders to hold individuals accountable for their performance. By setting performance standards and conducting regular evaluations, leaders ensure that team members meet their responsibilities and contribute effectively to the organization. For example, a department head might use their authority to conduct performance reviews, provide feedback, and implement improvement plans for underperforming employees.

The Importance of Collaboration in Leadership

While authority is necessary, collaboration is equally important in creating a thriving organizational culture. Collaboration involves working together, sharing ideas, and leveraging the diverse skills and perspectives of team members to achieve common goals. A collaborative environment encourages innovation, improves problem-solving, and fosters a sense of ownership among team members.

1. Encouraging Open Communication

Collaboration begins with open communication. Leaders who foster a collaborative environment encourage team members to share their ideas, provide feedback, and engage in meaningful discussions. For example, a team leader might hold regular brainstorming sessions where team members can contribute ideas and solutions. This approach not only generates a wealth of ideas but also makes team members feel valued and heard.

2. Empowering Team Members

Collaboration involves empowering team members to take ownership of their work and make decisions within their areas of expertise. This empowerment fosters a sense of responsibility and encourages individuals to contribute their best efforts. For instance, a leader might delegate decision-making authority to a team member who has specialized knowledge in a particular area. By doing so, the leader not only leverages the team member's expertise but also builds trust and confidence within the team.

3. Building Strong Relationships

Collaborative leaders focus on building strong relationships within the team. They recognize that trust and mutual respect are the foundations of effective collaboration. For example, a manager might take the time to get to know each team member personally, understanding their strengths, motivations, and challenges. This relationship-building creates a supportive environment where team members are more likely to collaborate and support each other.

Balancing Authority and Collaboration

The key to effective leadership lies in finding the right balance between authority and collaboration. Leaders must know when to assert their authority and when to step back and encourage collaboration. This balance is dynamic and may shift depending on the situation, the team's needs, and the organizational context.

1. Situational Leadership

Situational leadership involves adapting one's leadership style to the needs of the team and the demands of the situation. For example, during a crisis, a leader may need to take a more authoritative approach to make quick decisions and provide clear direction. In contrast, during the planning phase of a project, the same leader might adopt a more collaborative approach, seeking input from team members and encouraging open discussion.

2. Shared Decision-Making

Leaders can balance authority and collaboration by involving team members in decision-making processes. Shared decision-making allows team members to contribute their insights and expertise while the leader retains the final say. For instance, a department head might involve the team in developing a new strategy, gathering input and feedback before making the final decision. This approach ensures that the decision is informed by diverse perspectives while still maintaining the leader's authority.

3. Creating a Collaborative Culture with Clear Boundaries

To achieve a balance, leaders can create a collaborative culture with clear boundaries. This involves setting the ground rules for collaboration, defining the roles and responsibilities of each team member, and establishing decision-making protocols. For example, in a software development team, the project manager might encourage collaboration during the brainstorming and design phases but assert authority when making final decisions on project timelines and resource allocation.

4. Leading by Example

Leaders can also balance authority and collaboration by leading by example. This means demonstrating the behaviors they expect from their team members, such as open communication, respect for others' opinions, and a willingness to collaborate. For example, a leader who actively seeks input from team members, listens to their concerns, and values their contributions sets a positive example for the rest of the team to follow.

Example 1: Balancing Authority and Collaboration in a Tech Startup

In a tech startup, the CEO recognized the need for both authority and collaboration to drive innovation and growth.

While the CEO retained authority over the company's strategic direction, they encouraged a collaborative culture by empowering employees to take ownership of their projects and make decisions within their areas of expertise. The CEO also held regular town hall meetings where employees could share their ideas and feedback. This balance allowed the startup to remain agile and innovative while maintaining clear leadership and direction.

Example 2: A Collaborative Approach in Healthcare

In a hospital setting, a department head faced the challenge of implementing a new patient care protocol. The head used their authority to set the expectations and timelines for the new protocol but involved the entire team in the planning and execution phases. By seeking input from doctors, nurses, and administrative staff, the department head ensured that the protocol was practical and met the needs of all stakeholders. This collaborative approach led to a smoother implementation and higher staff engagement.

PART V: SUSTAINING LONG-TERM LEADERSHIP

CONTINUOUS IMPROVEMENT AS A LEADER

Developing a growth mindset is essential for sustaining long-term leadership. A growth mindset, as defined by psychologist Carol Dweck, is the belief that abilities and intelligence can be developed through dedication, hard work, and continuous learning. Leaders with a growth mindset are more likely to embrace challenges, persist in the face of setbacks, and see effort as a path to mastery. This mindset is not only crucial for personal development but also for inspiring and leading others effectively over the long term.

DEVELOPING A GROWTH MINDSET

A growth mindset is foundational for effective leadership because it shapes how leaders perceive their own abilities and those of others. Leaders with a growth mindset believe that talent and intelligence are just the starting points. They understand that improvement is possible through effort, learning, and perseverance. This belief empowers them to take on challenges, learn from failures, and continually improve their leadership skills.

1. Encourages Continuous Learning

Leaders with a growth mindset are committed to lifelong learning. They seek out new knowledge, skills, and experiences that can enhance their leadership abilities. Continuous learning is vital in a rapidly changing world where leaders must adapt to new challenges and technologies. For example, a leader who regularly reads industry-related books, attends workshops, or seeks mentorship is more likely to stay ahead of trends and make informed decisions.

2. Fosters Resilience in the Face of Challenges

Challenges are inevitable in leadership, but those with a growth mindset view challenges as opportunities for growth rather than threats. This perspective fosters resilience, enabling leaders to persist through difficulties and setbacks. For instance, a CEO who faces a major business downturn might see it as a chance to innovate and pivot the company's strategy, rather than as an insurmountable obstacle.

3. Promotes Adaptability to Change

In today's fast-paced environment, adaptability is crucial for leadership success. Leaders with a growth mindset are more open to change and are willing to adjust their strategies and approaches when necessary. They are not rigid in their thinking but are flexible and responsive to new information and circumstances. For example, a manager who embraces digital transformation in their organization is likely to succeed by adapting to new technologies and processes.

Strategies for Developing a Growth Mindset

Cultivating a growth mindset requires deliberate effort and practice. Here are several strategies that can help leaders develop and sustain a growth mindset:

1. Embrace Lifelong Learning

Lifelong learning is at the heart of a growth mindset. Leaders should make it a habit to continuously seek new knowledge and skills. This can be achieved through formal education, such as enrolling in courses or pursuing advanced degrees, as well as informal learning, such as reading, networking, and learning from peers. Leaders can also benefit from seeking feedback from others, as this provides valuable insights into areas for improvement.

Example: Satya Nadella

Satya Nadella, CEO of Microsoft, is known for his commitment to lifelong learning. Under his leadership, Microsoft underwent a cultural transformation that emphasized continuous learning and growth. Nadella's growth mindset allowed him to steer the company towards innovation and success in the rapidly changing tech industry.

2. Reframe Challenges as Opportunities

Leaders with a growth mindset view challenges as opportunities to learn and grow. Instead of avoiding difficult situations, they embrace them as chances to develop new skills and gain valuable experience. Reframing challenges in this way can help leaders approach problems with a positive attitude and a willingness to persevere.

Example: Howard Schultz

Howard Schultz, former CEO of Starbucks, faced numerous challenges in his career, including the decision to close underperforming stores during the 2008 financial crisis. Instead of seeing this as a failure, Schultz viewed it as an opportunity to refocus and strengthen the company. His growth mindset helped Starbucks recover and thrive in the years that followed.

3. Cultivate Resilience

Resilience is the ability to bounce back from setbacks and keep moving forward. Leaders with a growth mindset understand that failures and setbacks are part of the learning process. They use these experiences to build resilience and develop the mental toughness needed to lead effectively.

Example: Oprah Winfrey

Oprah Winfrey is a prime example of resilience. Despite facing numerous obstacles and setbacks throughout her career, she persisted and became one of the most successful media moguls in the world. Her growth mindset allowed her to learn from her experiences and continuously improve her craft.

4. Encourage a Culture of Feedback

Feedback is essential for growth, as it provides leaders with the information they need to improve. Leaders with a growth mindset actively seek feedback and encourage others to do the same. By fostering a culture of feedback within their teams, leaders can create an environment where continuous improvement is valued and supported.

Example: Ray Dalio

Ray Dalio, founder of Bridgewater Associates, is known for promoting a culture of feedback within his organization. Dalio believes that honest feedback is crucial for personal and organizational growth. This approach has helped Bridgewater become one of the most successful hedge funds in the world.

5. Focus on Effort, Not Just Outcomes

Leaders with a growth mindset recognize the importance of effort in achieving success. They focus on the process of learning and improving, rather than solely on the outcomes. By valuing effort, leaders can motivate themselves and their teams to keep striving for excellence, even when immediate results are not visible.

Example: Serena Williams

Serena Williams, one of the greatest tennis players of all time, exemplifies the importance of effort in achieving success. Throughout her career, Williams has focused on continuous improvement, putting in countless hours of practice and training to stay at the top of her game. Her growth mindset has been a key factor in her sustained success.

6. Embrace Failure as a Learning Tool

Failure is an inevitable part of leadership, but leaders with a growth mindset view failure as a valuable learning tool. Instead of being discouraged by failure, they analyze what went wrong, learn from the experience, and apply those lessons to future challenges.

Example: Steve Jobs

Steve Jobs, co-founder of Apple, experienced a major failure when he was ousted from the company he helped create. However, Jobs used this setback as an opportunity to learn and grow. He went on to lead successful ventures like Pixar and eventually returned to Apple, where he transformed the company into one of the most innovative and successful in the world.

7. Develop a Reflective Practice

Reflection is a powerful tool for developing a growth mindset. Leaders should regularly reflect on their experiences, identify areas for improvement, and set goals for personal development. Keeping a journal, engaging in self-assessment, or seeking feedback from mentors can help leaders cultivate a reflective practice.

Example: Angela Merkel

Angela Merkel, former Chancellor of Germany, is known for her thoughtful and reflective leadership style. Throughout her tenure, Merkel regularly reflected on her decisions and sought input from advisors to continuously improve her leadership approach. Her growth mindset contributed to her long-standing success as one of the world's most influential leaders.

The Impact of a Growth Mindset on Leadership

Leaders who cultivate a growth mindset are better equipped to navigate the complexities of leadership and drive long-term success. The impact of a growth mindset extends beyond personal development; it also influences the culture and performance of the entire organization.

1. Inspires a Culture of Continuous Improvement

Leaders with a growth mindset inspire their teams to adopt the same attitude towards learning and development. By modeling continuous improvement and encouraging others to do the same, leaders can create a culture where growth and innovation are valued. This culture of continuous improvement leads to higher levels of engagement, creativity, and performance within the organization.

2. Enhances Innovation and Adaptability

A growth mindset fosters innovation by encouraging leaders and their teams to explore new ideas, take risks, and learn from mistakes. In an environment where experimentation is encouraged, teams are more likely to develop innovative solutions to complex problems. Additionally, a growth mindset enhances adaptability, enabling leaders and their teams to respond effectively to changes in the external environment.

3. Builds Stronger, More Resilient Teams

Leaders with a growth mindset build stronger, more resilient teams by fostering a sense of psychological safety, where team members feel comfortable taking risks and sharing their ideas. This resilience is crucial for navigating challenges and maintaining high performance in the face of adversity.

Example: Jeff Bezos

Jeff Bezos, founder of Amazon, has consistently demonstrated a growth mindset throughout his career. His willingness to experiment, take risks, and learn from failures has driven Amazon's relentless innovation and growth. Under Bezos's leadership, Amazon has become one of the most successful companies in the world, known for its adaptability and customer-centric approach.

STAYING ADAPTABLE IN A CHANGING ENVIRONMENT

In a rapidly changing environment, adaptability is a critical skill for leaders. The ability to anticipate, respond to, and navigate change effectively can determine the success or failure of an organization. As a change management expert, I'll guide you through the key strategies leaders can use to stay adaptable in dynamic situations. This involves anticipating changes, maintaining flexibility, and adjusting strategies as needed. I'll also provide real-world examples of leaders who have thrived in such environments.

The Importance of Anticipating Change

Anticipating change is the first step in staying adaptable. Leaders who can foresee potential shifts in the market, technology, or societal trends are better positioned to respond proactively rather than reactively. Anticipation allows leaders to prepare their organizations for change, reducing the impact of disruptions and seizing opportunities before competitors.

1. Environmental Scanning

Environmental scanning involves regularly monitoring external factors that could impact the organization. This includes keeping an eye on industry trends, economic indicators, technological advancements, and regulatory changes. By staying informed, leaders can identify potential changes early and develop strategies to address them. For example, a retail company might monitor emerging e-commerce trends and consumer behavior shifts to anticipate changes in customer purchasing habits.

2. Scenario Planning

Scenario planning is a strategic tool that allows leaders to consider various future scenarios and their potential impact on the organization. By developing multiple scenarios, leaders can explore different possibilities and prepare for a range of outcomes. For instance, a manufacturing company might create scenarios for supply chain disruptions due to geopolitical tensions or natural disasters, allowing them to develop contingency plans for each scenario.

Example: Jeff Bezos

Jeff Bezos, the founder of Amazon, is known for his ability to anticipate changes in the market. Early on, Bezos recognized the potential of e-commerce and invested heavily in building Amazon's online infrastructure. His foresight allowed Amazon to become the dominant player in online retail, and he continues to anticipate market shifts, such as the growing demand for cloud computing and artificial intelligence.

Staying Flexible in a Changing Environment

Flexibility is essential for leaders who need to adapt to new situations quickly. A flexible leader can pivot their strategy, restructure their organization, or adopt new technologies without getting stuck in outdated practices. Flexibility allows leaders to respond to change in real time, minimizing disruptions and maintaining momentum.

1. Agile Leadership

Agile leadership involves adopting an iterative approach to decision-making and problem-solving. Instead of rigidly adhering to a single plan, agile leaders are open to experimentation and incremental improvements. They value feedback from their teams and are willing to make adjustments as needed. For example, a software development team might use agile methodologies, such as Scrum, to continuously refine their product based on user feedback.

2. Empowering Teams

Flexibility also involves empowering teams to make decisions and take action without waiting for top-down directives. When teams are given the autonomy to respond to changes on the ground, they can adapt more quickly to new challenges and opportunities. A leader who fosters a culture of empowerment encourages creativity and innovation, allowing the organization to stay ahead of the curve.

Example: Satya Nadella

Satya Nadella, CEO of Microsoft, exemplifies flexible leadership. When he took over as CEO, Microsoft was facing challenges in a rapidly changing tech landscape. Nadella embraced a more agile approach, shifting Microsoft's focus to cloud computing and open-source technology. By fostering a culture of collaboration and empowerment, Nadella was able to lead Microsoft through a successful transformation, revitalizing the company's growth.

Adjusting Strategies as Needed

Adapting to change often requires leaders to adjust their strategies. This might involve revisiting organizational goals, reallocating resources, or even redefining the company's mission. Leaders who can adapt their strategies in response to change are more likely to achieve long-term success.

1. Continuous Learning and Development

Leaders must be committed to continuous learning and development to stay adaptable. This involves not only keeping up with industry trends but also seeking out new knowledge and skills. By staying curious and open to new ideas, leaders can identify opportunities for strategic adjustments. For example, a leader might take courses on digital transformation or attend industry conferences to learn about emerging trends that could impact their organization.

2. Data-Driven Decision-Making

In a rapidly changing environment, data-driven decision-making is crucial. Leaders should leverage data analytics to gain insights into market trends, customer behavior, and operational performance. By making decisions based on data, rather than gut instincts, leaders can more accurately adjust their strategies to align with current realities. For instance, a marketing team might use data analytics to adjust their campaign strategy based on real-time customer feedback.

3. Communicating Change Effectively

Adjusting strategies often involves significant organizational changes, which can be challenging for employees. Effective communication is key to ensuring that everyone understands the reasons for the change and how it will impact them. Leaders should be transparent about the need for adjustments and provide clear guidance on how the organization will move forward. This helps to build trust and buy-in from employees, making the transition smoother.

Example: Howard Schultz

Howard Schultz, former CEO of Starbucks, demonstrated the ability to adjust strategies effectively. During the 2008 financial crisis, Schultz made the difficult decision to close underperforming stores and refocus the company's efforts on quality and customer experience. By adjusting Starbucks' strategy and communicating the changes clearly to employees and customers, Schultz was able to navigate the company through a challenging period and restore its profitability.

Thriving in Dynamic Situations

Leaders who can anticipate change, stay flexible, and adjust their strategies are well-equipped to thrive in dynamic situations. These leaders not only respond to change but also leverage it as an opportunity for growth and innovation. By staying adaptable, they can lead their organizations to success, even in the face of uncertainty.

1. Embracing a Growth Mindset

Thriving in a rapidly changing environment requires a growth mindset, where leaders see challenges as opportunities for learning and development. Leaders with a growth mindset are more likely to take risks, experiment with new ideas, and embrace change as a natural part of the business landscape. This mindset fosters resilience and allows leaders to adapt to new situations with confidence.

2. Building a Resilient Organization

Resilient organizations are better able to withstand and adapt to change. Leaders can build resilience by fostering a strong organizational culture, investing in employee development, and creating flexible systems and processes. By prioritizing resilience, leaders ensure that their organizations can weather storms and emerge stronger on the other side.

3. Leading with Vision and Purpose

Leaders who thrive in dynamic environments often have a clear vision and purpose that guides their decisions. This vision provides a sense of direction and stability, even when external circumstances are uncertain. By staying focused on their long-term goals, leaders can navigate short-term challenges without losing sight of the bigger picture.

Example: Elon Musk

Elon Musk, CEO of Tesla and SpaceX, is a prime example of a leader who thrives in dynamic situations. Musk's ability to anticipate future trends, such as the rise of electric vehicles and space exploration, has allowed him to lead groundbreaking innovations. His flexibility in adapting strategies, such as shifting Tesla's focus to renewable energy solutions, has been instrumental in the success of his ventures. Musk's growth mindset and visionary leadership have enabled him to navigate the complexities of the tech industry and drive transformative change.

MEASURING THE IMPACT OF YOUR LEADERSHIP

Measuring the impact of your leadership through self-assessment and reflection is crucial for continuous growth and effectiveness. As a leadership development expert, I'll guide you through the process of using self-assessment tools and reflection techniques to evaluate your leadership impact, set measurable goals, and foster meaningful improvements. This guide will cover various assessment methods, the importance of feedback, and examples of effective self-assessment practices.

TOOLS FOR SELF-ASSESSMENT AND REFLECTION

Self-assessment is a critical aspect of leadership development. It allows leaders to gain insight into their strengths and weaknesses, understand how their behavior affects others, and identify areas for improvement. Regular self-assessment ensures that leaders remain aware of their impact and can make informed decisions about their development.

Self-assessment also encourages accountability. By regularly reflecting on your leadership style and effectiveness, you take ownership of your growth and are more likely to stay committed to continuous improvement. Moreover, self-assessment fosters a growth mindset, where leaders see challenges as opportunities for learning and development.

Tools for Self-Assessment

Several tools can help leaders assess their impact and effectiveness. These tools provide structured methods for evaluating leadership skills, behaviors, and outcomes. Below are some common self-assessment tools:

1. 360-Degree Feedback

Overview: 360-degree feedback involves collecting feedback from various sources, including peers, subordinates, superiors, and sometimes even customers. This method provides a comprehensive view of your leadership impact from multiple perspectives.

Benefits: This approach offers a well-rounded assessment of your leadership style and effectiveness. It highlights blind spots and areas for improvement that you may not be aware of.

How to Use: After receiving feedback, identify common themes and areas where your perception differs from others. Use this information to set specific, measurable goals for improvement.

Example: A team leader in a corporate setting might receive feedback that, while they excel at driving results, they could improve their communication and empathy towards team members. This insight allows them to focus on enhancing their interpersonal skills.

2. Self-Reflection Journals

Overview: Keeping a self-reflection journal is a simple yet powerful tool for self-assessment. By regularly writing about your experiences, decisions, and outcomes, you can gain deeper insights into your leadership style and effectiveness.

Benefits: Journaling encourages introspection and helps you identify patterns in your behavior and decision-making processes. It also provides a record of your leadership journey, allowing you to track your progress over time.

How to Use: Set aside time daily or weekly to reflect on your leadership experiences. Consider questions such as: What went well? What could I have done differently? How did my actions impact others?

Example: A school principal might use a reflection journal to analyze how their decisions affect student outcomes and staff morale, helping them refine their leadership approach.

3. Leadership Competency Frameworks

Overview: Leadership competency frameworks outline the skills and behaviors expected of effective leaders. These frameworks can be used as a self-assessment tool to evaluate your competencies against established benchmarks.

Benefits: This method provides a clear structure for assessing your leadership abilities and identifying areas for development. It also aligns your self-assessment with organizational expectations.

How to Use: Review the competencies outlined in the framework and rate yourself on each one. Identify gaps between your current skills and the desired competencies, and create a development plan to address these gaps.

Example: A healthcare manager might use a leadership competency framework to assess their skills in areas such as decision-making, patient care, and team collaboration, leading to targeted development efforts.

4. Behavioral Assessment Tools

Overview: Behavioral assessments, such as the DISC or Myers-Briggs Type Indicator (MBTI), provide insights into your personality traits and how they influence your leadership style.

Benefits: Understanding your behavioral tendencies can help you identify how you interact with others, manage conflict, and make decisions. This awareness enables you to adjust your behavior to enhance your leadership effectiveness.

How to Use: After completing the assessment, review the results and consider how your personality traits impact your leadership. Use this information to develop strategies for leveraging your strengths and addressing potential weaknesses.

Example: A project manager who learns they have a preference for introversion through the MBTI might focus on improving their visibility and communication with their team.

The Role of Feedback in Self-Assessment

Feedback is a vital component of self-assessment. While self-reflection is essential, feedback from others provides an external perspective that can validate or challenge your self-assessment. Feedback helps you understand how others perceive your leadership and offers insights that you might not have considered.

1. Seeking Feedback Regularly

To get the most out of feedback, make it a regular practice to seek input from others. This could be through formal mechanisms, like 360-degree feedback, or informal conversations with colleagues and team members.

Be open to both positive and constructive feedback. While it's natural to focus on areas for improvement, recognizing your strengths is equally important for reinforcing effective behaviors.

2. Creating a Feedback Culture

Encourage a culture of feedback within your organization or team. When feedback is normalized and valued, people are more likely to provide honest and constructive insights. As a leader, model this behavior by regularly giving and receiving feedback.

Create safe spaces where team members feel comfortable sharing their thoughts. This can be achieved by fostering trust and demonstrating that feedback leads to positive changes.

Example: A department head might schedule regular one-on-one meetings with team members to discuss their performance and ask for feedback on their own leadership. This not only provides valuable insights but also strengthens relationships within the team.

Setting Measurable Leadership Goals

After assessing your leadership impact through self-assessment and feedback, the next step is to set measurable goals for improvement. Measurable goals are specific, quantifiable, and time-bound, making it easier to track progress and stay motivated.

1. Setting SMART Goals

SMART goals are Specific, Measurable, Achievable, Relevant, and Time-bound. This framework ensures that your leadership goals are clear and actionable.

Specific: Clearly define what you want to achieve. For example, instead of saying "improve communication," set a specific goal like "increase team meeting participation by 20%."

Measurable: Establish criteria to measure your progress. For example, use surveys or feedback forms to track changes in team engagement.

Achievable: Ensure your goals are realistic and attainable. Consider your current resources, time, and support systems.

Relevant: Align your goals with your broader leadership objectives and the organization's mission.

Time-bound: Set a deadline for achieving your goals to create a sense of urgency and focus.

Example: A sales director might set a SMART goal to "Increase quarterly sales by 15% by implementing a new customer relationship management (CRM) strategy within the next six months."

2. Breaking down Goals into Actionable Steps

Once you've set your goals, break them down into smaller, actionable steps. This makes it easier to manage your progress and avoid feeling overwhelmed.

Identify the resources, support, and time needed for each step. Assign deadlines for each action to keep yourself on track.

Example: If your goal is to improve team communication, actionable steps might include scheduling regular team check-ins, providing communication training, and implementing a feedback loop.

3. Monitoring Progress and Adjusting Goals

Regularly monitor your progress toward your goals. Use self-assessment tools and feedback to evaluate your achievements and identify any areas where you may need to adjust your approach.

Be flexible in adjusting your goals as circumstances change. If you encounter obstacles or if priorities shift, reassess your goals and make the necessary adjustments to stay aligned with your overall objectives.

Example: A nonprofit leader might set a goal to increase community engagement by 30% through outreach programs. If they find that certain strategies are not yielding the desired results, they might adjust their approach by exploring new outreach channels or refining their messaging.

Examples of Effective Self-Assessment Practices

To illustrate the effectiveness of self-assessment and reflection, let's explore a few examples of leaders who have successfully used these practices to enhance their leadership impact.

1. Sheryl Sandberg: Self-Reflection and Feedback

Sheryl Sandberg, COO of Facebook, is known for her commitment to self-reflection and feedback. Throughout her career, Sandberg has actively sought feedback from colleagues and mentors to gain insights into her leadership style. By regularly reflecting on this feedback, she has been able to refine her approach, improve her decision-making, and become a more effective leader. Sandberg's emphasis on self-assessment has contributed to her success in leading one of the world's most influential tech companies.

2. Satya Nadella: Continuous Learning and Adaptation

Satya Nadella, CEO of Microsoft, has demonstrated the power of continuous learning and adaptation in leadership. When Nadella took over as CEO, he recognized the need to shift Microsoft's focus to cloud computing and artificial intelligence. Through regular self-assessment and reflection, Nadella was able to identify areas where he needed to develop new skills and knowledge. By committing to continuous learning, he successfully led Microsoft through a period of significant transformation, resulting in the company's resurgence as a global tech leader.

3. Howard Schultz: Visionary Leadership and Feedback

Howard Schultz, former CEO of Starbucks, has long been an advocate for visionary leadership. However, Schultz's success also stems from his commitment to seeking feedback and using self-assessment to align his leadership with the company's mission. Schultz regularly engaged with employees and customers to understand their perspectives, allowing him to make informed decisions that resonated with stakeholders. His ability to balance vision with feedback-driven decision-making helped Starbucks become a global leader in the coffee industry.

CREATING A LEGACY WITHOUT FORMAL AUTHORITY

Creating a lasting impact and legacy within an organization doesn't require a formal leadership title. A true legacy is built on influence, values, and the contributions you make that resonate beyond your tenure. As a leadership legacy expert, I'll outline how you can establish a lasting legacy through mentoring others, driving long-term initiatives, and embedding your values into the organizational culture, even without holding an official leadership position.

Understanding Legacy beyond Titles

Legacy is about the long-term impact you leave on people, processes, and culture. While titles come and go, the influence you exert through your actions, relationships, and the values you champion endures. A legacy is defined not by the position you hold but by how you make a difference and the positive changes you inspire within your organization.

Mentoring Others: Building a Legacy through People

One of the most powerful ways to create a lasting legacy is through mentoring others. Mentorship allows you to pass on your knowledge, skills, and values to the next generation of leaders, ensuring that your influence continues to shape the organization even after you've moved on.

1. Identifying and Developing Talent

Start by identifying individuals within your organization who show potential but might lack the experience or confidence to step into leadership roles. Take the initiative to offer guidance, support, and opportunities for them to grow. By investing in their development, you're not only helping them succeed but also ensuring that your approach to leadership and problem-solving is perpetuated.

2. Leading by Example

Mentorship isn't just about giving advice; it's about modeling the behaviors and values you want to see in others. Demonstrate integrity, commitment, and a strong work ethic in everything you do. Your mentees are more likely to adopt these qualities when they see them consistently exemplified in your actions.

3. Creating a Mentorship Culture

To create a lasting legacy, consider how you can institutionalize mentorship within your organization. Advocate for formal mentoring programs, encourage others to take on mentoring roles, and foster an environment where knowledge-sharing is valued. A mentorship culture not only develops individual talent but also strengthens the overall organizational fabric.

Example: Maya Angelou

Maya Angelou, a renowned author and civil rights activist, created a lasting legacy not through a formal leadership title but through her mentorship of others. She inspired countless individuals through her wisdom, encouragement, and example. Her influence can be seen in the lives of those she mentored, such as Oprah Winfrey, who has often spoken about Angelou's impact on her life and career.

Driving Long-Term Initiatives: Leaving a Mark on the Organization

Another way to build a legacy is by spearheading long-term initiatives that align with your values and the organization's goals. Even without a formal title, you can take the lead on projects that have a lasting impact.

1. Identifying Opportunities for Improvement

Look for areas within the organization where you can make a difference. This could involve improving processes, advocating for new technologies, or championing sustainability initiatives.

By focusing on areas that align with your expertise and passion, you're more likely to drive meaningful change.

2. Collaborating Across Departments

To successfully drive long-term initiatives, it's essential to collaborate with others across the organization. Building alliances and working together towards common goals not only enhances the impact of your initiatives but also ensures they are embraced by a wider audience. Collaboration also demonstrates your ability to lead without formal authority.

3. Measuring and Communicating Impact

Track the progress and outcomes of the initiatives you lead. This not only helps you adjust your approach as needed but also provides evidence of your contributions to the organization. Regularly communicate the impact of these initiatives to stakeholders, ensuring that your efforts are recognized and valued.

Example: Malala Yousafzai

Malala Yousafzai, a Pakistani activist for female education, has driven significant long-term initiatives without holding any formal leadership title. Through her advocacy and the Malala Fund, she has championed the right to education for girls worldwide. Her legacy continues to grow as her efforts influence global education policies and inspire others to join the cause.

Embedding Values into Organizational Culture: The True Measure of Legacy

A lasting legacy is deeply rooted in the values you embed within the organizational culture. These values guide behavior, decision-making, and the overall direction of the organization, long after you're gone.

1. Identifying Core Values

Reflect on the values that are most important to you and that you believe will benefit the organization in the long run. These might include integrity, innovation, inclusivity, or customer focus. Once identified, find ways to incorporate these values into your daily work and interactions.

2. Advocating for Value-Driven Decisions

Influence decision-making processes by consistently advocating for choices that align with your core values. Whether in meetings, project planning, or informal discussions, make it clear that values should drive the organization's actions. By doing so, you help to establish a culture where decisions are made not just based on short-term gains but on long-term principles.

3. Recognizing and Rewarding Value-Driven Behavior

Encourage others to embrace these values by recognizing and rewarding behavior that exemplifies them. This could involve nominating colleagues for awards, publicly acknowledging their contributions, or simply offering positive feedback. When values are celebrated, they become an integral part of the organizational culture.

Example: Mahatma Gandhi

Mahatma Gandhi, who held no formal political office, created a lasting legacy by embedding the values of nonviolence and truth into the fabric of Indian society and the global consciousness. His influence on civil rights movements worldwide demonstrates how deeply rooted values can transcend titles and positions, leaving an enduring legacy.

Case Studies: Individuals Who Have Created Significant Legacies without Formal Authority

1. Mother Teresa

Mother Teresa, the founder of the Missionaries of Charity, is a prime example of someone who created a lasting legacy without holding a formal leadership title. Her work with the poor and destitute in Kolkata, India, left an indelible mark on the world. Through her compassion, dedication, and unwavering commitment to service, she inspired millions and left a legacy of kindness and humanitarianism that continues to influence people globally.

2. Nelson Mandela

Before becoming the President of South Africa, Nelson Mandela had already established a powerful legacy through his activism against apartheid. Even while imprisoned, his influence grew as he became a symbol of resistance and hope. Mandela's ability to lead a nation towards reconciliation and unity after his release, without holding any formal power during much of his activism, demonstrates the profound impact one can have without a title.

3. Rosa Parks

Rosa Parks, known as "the mother of the civil rights movement," made history by refusing to give up her bus seat to a white man in Montgomery, Alabama. Although she held no formal leadership position, her courage sparked the Montgomery Bus Boycott and became a pivotal moment in the American civil rights movement. Parks' legacy is a testament to the power of individual action and its capacity to drive societal change.

CONCLUSION:

Measuring the impact of your leadership through self-assessment and reflection is an essential practice for continuous improvement and growth. As a leadership development expert, I'll guide you on how to effectively use self-assessment tools, gather feedback, and set measurable goals to enhance your leadership effectiveness.

Self-assessment is the first step in understanding your strengths and areas for improvement as a leader. It allows you to reflect on your actions, decisions, and the outcomes they produce, providing insight into how you can better serve your team and organization. Self-assessment can be conducted through various methods, each offering unique perspectives on your leadership abilities.

One common self-assessment method is the use of leadership questionnaires and surveys. These tools typically include a series of questions designed to evaluate different aspects of leadership, such as decision-making, communication, emotional intelligence, and team management. By answering these questions honestly, you can gain a clearer picture of your leadership style and identify areas where you may need to develop further. For example, a questionnaire might ask you to rate your ability to provide constructive feedback or your effectiveness in managing conflicts. Your responses can highlight whether these are areas of strength or opportunities for growth.

Another effective self-assessment method is reflective journaling. This involves regularly writing down your thoughts, experiences, and challenges related to your leadership role. By reflecting on these entries over time, you can identify patterns in your behavior, recognize recurring challenges, and gain deeper insights into your leadership journey. Reflective journaling encourages continuous learning and helps you track your progress in developing key leadership skills. For instance, if you notice that you frequently struggle with delegating tasks, you can focus on improving this skill and monitor your progress through subsequent journal entries.

360-degree feedback is a valuable tool that complements self-assessment by providing a comprehensive view of your leadership from multiple perspectives. This method involves gathering feedback from a variety of sources, including peers, subordinates, and superiors. The feedback typically covers various aspects of your leadership, such as communication, decision-making, and interpersonal relationships. The advantage of 360-degree feedback is that it offers a holistic view of your leadership, highlighting strengths and areas for improvement that you may not have been aware of. For example, you might receive feedback that, while you excel at strategic thinking, you need to improve your approachability with your team. This insight allows you to take targeted action to enhance your leadership effectiveness.

The importance of feedback in leadership cannot be overstated. Regular feedback helps you stay aware of how your leadership is perceived by others and allows you to make adjustments as needed. It's essential to create a culture of open and honest communication where feedback is welcomed and valued. To encourage this, consider implementing regular check-ins with your team, where you can discuss your leadership approach and invite feedback. This not only helps you improve but also demonstrates your commitment to continuous development and fosters trust within your team.

Setting measurable leadership goals is a crucial component of self-assessment and reflection. Clear, specific goals provide a roadmap for your leadership development and allow you to track your progress over time. When setting goals, it's important to ensure they are SMART: Specific, Measurable, Achievable, Relevant, and Time-bound. For example, instead of setting a vague goal like "improve communication," a SMART goal would be "conduct weekly team meetings where I actively listen to all members and provide constructive feedback, and review progress after three months."

Measurable goals also enable you to assess the impact of your leadership on your team and organization. For instance, if one of your goals is to increase team productivity, you can track key performance indicators (KPIs) such as project completion rates, team efficiency, and employee engagement. By regularly reviewing these metrics, you can determine whether your leadership efforts are having the desired effect and make adjustments if necessary.

Effective self-assessment and reflection also involve recognizing and celebrating your successes. Acknowledging your achievements helps build confidence and reinforces positive leadership behaviors. It's important to take time to reflect on what you've done well and consider how you can build on these successes. For example, if you successfully led a project that exceeded expectations, reflect on the strategies you used and how you can apply them to future initiatives.

In addition to self-assessment tools, engaging in leadership coaching or mentoring can provide valuable external perspectives on your leadership development. A coach or mentor can offer guidance, challenge your assumptions, and help you see blind spots that you might overlook in self-assessment. They can also assist you in setting realistic goals and developing action plans to achieve them. For example, a mentor with experience in your industry might provide insights into effective leadership strategies that you can incorporate into your own practice.

Case studies of successful leaders who have used self-assessment and reflection to enhance their leadership can serve as powerful examples. Consider the case of Indra Nooyi, former CEO of PepsiCo, who was known for her reflective approach to leadership. Nooyi regularly sought feedback from her peers and team members, which helped her identify areas for improvement and adapt her leadership style accordingly. Her commitment to continuous learning and self-assessment contributed to her success in leading PepsiCo through significant growth and innovation.

Another example is Alan Mulally, former CEO of Ford Motor Company. Mulally implemented a practice of weekly "business plan review" meetings, where he and his leadership team would assess the company's progress and make necessary adjustments. This regular self-assessment allowed Ford to navigate the challenges of the 2008 financial crisis and emerge as a stronger, more competitive company.

BONUS

Use your smartphone camera or a QR code scanning app to scan the code.

IPhone Users: Open your Camera app, point it at the QR code, and tap the link that appears.

Android Users: Open your Camera app or use a QR scanner app, then follow the link that pops up.

After scanning, you'll be directed to a webpage with your exclusive downloadable worksheets and templates.

www.ingramcontent.com/pod-product-compliance
Lightning Source LLC
Chambersburg PA
CBHW052140220526
45471CB00004B/1464